In memory of my father, Charles Edward Ethridge, who taught me to see the beauty in life.

Barbara Radke Blake

Dedicated to my mother, Dorothy Waxman Cohen, for her constant love.

Barbara Stein

CONTENTS

ACKNOWLEDGMENTS

The authors wish to recognize the following people for their assistance in the production of this book: Pat Schuman for conceptualizing and recognizing the need for this series; Margo Hart for being supportive and available at all times throughout the preparation of the manuscript; and Nancy Viggiano for her editorial assistance.

Our thanks to Kay Lincycomb for interlibrary loan service; to the University of North Texas Center of Instructional Services for graphics support; and to those who provided samples of public and school newsletters.

To Kathryn Connell and Larry Muirhead, thanks for encouragement when the project seemed overwhelming.

Our special thanks and appreciation to Billy Radke for his understanding, sense of humor, support, suggestions—and especially for providing (on request) popcorn and hot primavera pizzas in spite of rain, sleet, and snow!

Barbara Radke Blake

Barbara Stein

INTRODUCTION

Librarians face the ever-escalating challenge of doing more with less. This series of *How-To-Do-It Manuals for School and Public Librarians* is designed to provide librarians with practical tips for fulfilling a variety of responsibilities with increased efficiency and decreased expenditure. Combining technology with traditional techniques, the manuals enable library practitioners to take advantage of the myriad resources available to assist them in providing quality service to users at a reasonable cost.

Many librarians realize the value of a library newsletter, yet are uncertain about how to produce one. A newsletter advertises you and your organization every time it is seen or read. Promotional pieces (brochures, pamphlets, and flyers) are excellent public relations tools, too, and offer quick, useful information to library users. *Creating Newsletters, Brochures, and Pamphlets: A How-To-Do-It Manual for Librarians* dispels the mystery surrounding the design and production of newsletters and promotional pieces. While it is written to help the novice, more experienced newsletter editors will also profit from it.

Are you on a shoestring budget—or do you have ample funds available? Either way, proper planning can make the most of your resources. The first three chapters help you make planning decisions, including goals, budget, and design.

Chapters 4 through 6 provide ideas, tips, and techniques for gathering news as well as writing, editing, and proofing copy.

Chapters 7 and 8 explain how to produce a newsletter, whether you have only a typewriter or a full-blown desktop publishing setup.

Chapters 9 and 10 offer step-by-step instructions on how to lay out and paste up the final copy.

Chapter 11 explains how to develop a positive image for your publications.

Chapter 12 covers how to apply for bulk mailing rates.

The appendixes supplement the information in the body of the book with sources for microcomputer resources, sample bulk mail forms, standard proofreader symbols, and sample newsletters. Uncertain about punctuation and other questions of grammar? Never fear. Appendix E includes a directory of grammar hotlines.

Whether you have a one-person library or a staff of 20, *Creating Newsletters, Brochures, and Pamphlets* can help you to develop a positive image for your library.

1 GETTING STARTED

"In the beginning . . ."

You have no time, no staff, and no money. How can you produce effective publications? Should you produce a newsletter, a brochure, or a pamphlet? Ask yourself the following questions before deciding to publish a newsletter:

- Is a newsletter the best way to communicate, or should you inaugurate a column in an existing publication such as a local newspaper or the school paper if you are in a school?
- Is there enough pertinent information to justify publishing a newsletter on a continuing basis?
- Who will read it?
- Will it complement or replace meetings with teachers or with other groups?
- Are there alternative funds available from groups such as the Friends of the Library or PTA to help cover costs?
- Do you have the equipment needed to produce the newsletter, or does another department own equipment you can use?
- Will you be doing all the work yourself, or can you recruit other staff or volunteers to assist you?
- Will outside help be required?
- Will your administration make a commitment to your efforts to publish a newsletter?

ANALYZE YOUR PURPOSE

Define the purpose of the newsletter in 25 words or less. Consider the following factors to help identify your goals:

- Who is your audience? Teachers, administrators, other staff, parents, school board members, and

Friends of the Library? Will you send copies to the Chamber of Commerce, officers of civic groups, or other social agencies in the community?

- What material will you publish? What will you cover and not cover? You might include new policies, acquisitions, anecdotes, statistics, unusual gifts, bestsellers, new personnel, humor, a letters to the editor column, and books that relate to community events.
- What sources will you use for news? Input from teachers, students, parents, administration, Friends, Library Board members, library advocates? Or will you use only library staff as news sources?
- What are the objectives of your newsletter? To inform others about library services? To educate them about the library's materials? To entertain them with a humorous article or column? To promote upcoming events or activities? Will you advocate, dissent, or remain objective when reporting news and events?
- How will the information in your newsletter differ from other publications read by people in your community?
- What image do you want to project for the library? Warm and inviting? Straightforward and factual? Lighthearted and breezy? Newsletters can be a tool for shaping attitudes if used properly.

The purpose and editorial content form the basis of your promise to your readership. Make sure the content of the newsletter fulfills that promise.

GETTING SUPPORT

If you encounter resistance—or mixed messages—from your administration, it may be necessary to sell them on the idea. If you've followed the steps outlined above, you will have a well-thought-out proposal to take to the administration.

You may choose to produce a one-page newsletter requiring only a computer and appropriate software such as WordPerfect. If you decided to produce a more complex publication, you may need to have your job description revised to include the responsibility and authority to set deadlines, solicit articles, arrange for photo sessions, make final design and production decisions, and develop and implement a budget for the newsletter.

CHARACTERISTICS OF GOOD NEWSLETTERS

Good newsletters are popular because they are a fast read, portable, and give the reader specific, pertinent information. They are also similar to personal letters in their style and commentary and fill a void left by the decline of lengthy correspondence between friends and relatives.

EXPLOITING GOOD DESIGN

Design elements that contribute to the popularity of newsletters include:

DESIGN ELEMENTS

8½-by-11-inches, folded

No ads

No covers

Short

Specialized

- Newsletters are normally 8½-by-11-inches after they are folded.
- Because they do not contain outside advertising, readers tend to have confidence in the objectivity of their editorial content.
- Unlike magazines, they do not have covers.
- They are rarely more than 12 to 16 pages in length, and often run only 4 to 8 pages.
- Frequently, the type runs all the way across the page (full measure) or is divided into two or three columns.
- Newsletters contain specialized, rather than general, information.

COMPOSITION

There are a number of methods of newsletter composition. The basic elements of newsletter design apply to each method. Your newsletter can be typed and copied on a mimeograph machine, computer-generated and professionally typeset, or anything in between.

It is more important to choose the approach that fits your schedule and budget than to produce an impressive document. A simple one-page newsletter can be as effective as a longer, more sophisticated publication. A well-designed, well-written newsletter can enhance the understanding, appreciation, and use of your library.

BROCHURES AND PAMPHLETS

The purpose of a brochure is to provide information about the library. One brochure might tell what professional materials are available for use; another might explain audiovisual services; a third might instruct readers on using the online catalog; and still another might present a brief history of the library or the origin of its name. Patrons appreciate receiving brochures after a tour. Or you might make pamphlets part of an orientation package for new staff.

Brochures can be written for a general or a specific audience. For example, you might have two sets of brochures covering programs for children—one that provides parents with an overview of the library's offerings, and a second series of brochures for teachers that gives detailed, in-depth information.

FLYERS

Flyers, notices, or single 8½-by-11-inch printed sheets have a different purpose. They are used to announce a particular event or to describe a service. They have a shorter life than that of a brochure or pamphlet.

CONCLUSION

After deciding to produce a newsletter, brochure, pamphlet, or flyer, you need to determine how much it will cost and how much time it will take. Chapter 2 presents factors to consider in planning your budget and analyzing your schedule.

2 PLANNING A BUDGET

"If you've got the money . . ."

POINTS TO CONSIDER

Time

Flexibility

Budget

Quality

Consider the following factors when analyzing your schedule and planning your budget:

- How much time will it take to produce the publication?
- How flexible can you be on your production schedule?
- What are the costs of producing the publication yourself, compared to hiring outside help?
- What level of quality do you want to achieve in producing the publication?

OPTIONS

You can handle newsletter production with little or no support staff by assuming the roles of editor, writer, typist, paste-up artist, printer, and distributor. Or you can pay for outside help.

You can produce a simple publication with only yourself and a typewriter. If you have access to a computer, you can more easily create a professional-looking publication. Or if funds are available and you want a "slick" product, you may choose to pay for outside help.

IN-HOUSE PRODUCTION OR PRINT SHOP?

Using a computer yourself may be the most cost-effective option, especially if you lack production experience and sophisticated equipment. A computer can make it possible for you to project a professional image for the library with limited time and money. When developing your budget, consider the costs involved in producing it yourself as compared to having a print shop produce it for you. The costs of using a commercial print shop will vary depending on a number of factors.

POINTS TO CONSIDER

Schedule

Paper

Mailing

Folds

Consider your production schedule. Printing costs may be lower for a monthly newsletter with a five-day printing turnaround time than a weekly one with a one-day turnaround. You pay a premium price for a shorter turnaround time.

The weight and color of paper you choose will have an impact on the printing costs. Higher quality paper costs more, as does colored paper. Usually a standard 60-pound white offset stock is sufficient.

If you need to mail your publication, your expenses will increase. You can mail your newsletter in an envelope. Or you can make it a self-mailer—which is a newsletter that has the mailing information printed on the last page. A self-mailer is usually folded and perhaps stapled, then mailed without an envelope.

The way it is folded will change the cost. If you have the

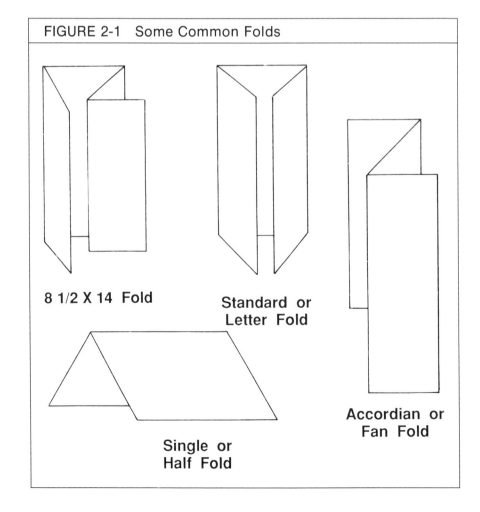

FIGURE 2-1   Some Common Folds

8 1/2 X 14 Fold

Standard or Letter Fold

Accordian or Fan Fold

Single or Half Fold

print shop fold it, you will be charged for the service. Fees vary for the different types of folds available.

Some common folds are the single or half fold, standard or letter fold, accordion or fan fold, and the 8½-by-14-inch fold. Figure 2-1 contains examples of each.

It costs less money (but more time) to fold it yourself. To achieve clean folds, use a folding bone. You can also purchase a folding machine, which is, however, expensive.

POINTS TO CONSIDER

Color

Copies

Interest

MORE COMMERCIAL OPTIONS

Two-color printing will increase costs since each sheet of paper has to be run through the printing press twice, once for each color. Black counts as a color.

While the number of copies you need to have made is an important consideration, print shops have a fixed standard for their set-up charges. These include making plates, preparing photos, inking the press, and cleaning it after the print run. These charges are constant, regardless of how many copies are run. Therefore, it is cheaper in terms of cost per copy to print a large number of copies. On the other hand, you will be paying for more paper. You may save money on paper, though, by offering to buy a six-month to one-year supply in advance, thus avoiding paper price increases and perhaps getting a bulk discount rate.

When selecting a print shop, take time to find one that is interested in printing a newsletter (not all of them are) and one that will do a good job of it. Ask to see samples of their work, and to speak with some of their newsletter clients.

FACTORS AFFECTING COSTS

Pages

Graphics

Reproduction

Staples

Holes

Duplex

Collate

OTHER BUDGET CONSIDERATIONS

Some other elements that affect the cost of producing a newsletter are:

- The number of pages, illustrations, or photos that will be used. Costs increase with additional graphics.
- The method of reproduction, whether mimeograph machine, photocopier, photo offset, or typeset. Typesetting can add about 50 percent to costs and days to the production schedule.
- Whether or not it will be stapled, since stapling adds to the overall cost, as does collating the pages.
- Having holes drilled in the newsletter for insertion into binders adds to costs, as does duplex copy (setting type on both sides of each sheet).

• Inflation. It's a good idea to add ten percent to the final figure since the price of paper continues to rise steadily.

COMPOSITION

Composition is the term used for preparing the newsletter for printing. Printing refers to the reproduction of the newsletter in quantity.

Methods of newsletter composition include using a typewriter, a word processor with a dot-matrix or daisy-wheel printer, a computer with desktop publishing and a laser printer, or typeset composition incorporating phototypesetting or digital typography.

TYPEWRITER

Using a typewriter is the least expensive and easiest method. Attractive and interesting typography can be achieved by using a machine with interchangeable type fonts. Another option, if your typewriter has unusually large type, is to type the copy on large sheets and have them reduced to 8½-by-11-inches. Of course, typewriters range in sophistication from the manual to the electronic memory typewriter. The electronic memory typewriter is a step up from the electric typewriter and a step below the personal computer in both cost and ease of use.

WORD PROCESSOR

A word processor offers ease of editing and text reorganization, as well as formatting flexibility. It enables you to produce a professional-looking newsletter economically.

A primary factor to consider when selecting word processing software is how the program handles files. Does it produce a series of pages that you have to repaginate if you change text? A series of lines that requires you to press "enter" after each line? Or a string of text that automatically inserts and displays the page breaks?

How closely the text on the screen resembles the final document is also important. WYSIWYG means "what you see is what you get" and is used for those programs that attempt to approximate the printed page on the computer screen. Other factors to consider are the modes of writing, editing, printing, and manipulating the cursor, and how the pages are formatted.

DESKTOP PUBLISHING

Desktop publishing offers tremendous versatility. You can create or import graphics, change type styles and size, and move and edit text. You can write your stories, implement your layout and design, and typeset the result. You can print the results on a dot-matrix printer, laser printer, or phototypesetter. Optical scanners can convert line art and photos into your own computer clip-art files—and there are commercially prepared electronic clip-art programs available as well.

REPRODUCTION

Mimeograph, photocopy, and photo offset are three methods of newsletter reproduction.

MIMEOGRAPH

Mimeographing is the least expensive method. You simply type directly onto a thin paper stencil (using correction fluid to make changes), then place the stencil on the mimeograph machine drum. Next, you crank a handle or push a button (depending on the machine) to make copies of the stencil. (You can also make stencils electronically and can put any kind of camera-ready composition onto a stencil.) You can use line drawings or clip-art on your paste-up; create headlines made with transfer type (rub-on letters); arrange your newsletter in columns; employ a variety of colored papers.

Purchase nonreproducible blue-lined layout pads to use in typing and layout. (The blue lines will not show when the page is copied.) You can also purchase multiple drums and use a different color with each one to achieve different print colors.

The main drawbacks to this method are that mimeograph copies are the poorest in quality and you will be limited to 8½-by-11-inch sheets rather than the normal 11-by-17-inch sheets associated with commercially printed newsletters. In addition, photos will not print well.

PHOTOCOPY

Photocopying produces higher quality copies with clearer print than a mimeograph machine. Costs vary depending on whether you make the copies in-house or at a print shop. It is, however, more expensive than mimeograph copies, and you will usually be limited to 8½-by-11-inch or 8½-by-14-inch sheets rather than the more common 11-by-17-inches used for a newsletter.

PHOTO OFFSET

Photo offset printing produces a better quality copy. Quick print shops use the offset negative method. Your paste-up pages of camera-ready copy are photographed, and a negative is made of the photo. A metal printing plate is then made from the negative, and copies of the page are run from the metal printing plate.

Camera-ready copy refers to pages that are in final form for reproduction. They require no further alteration or work and have been laid out and pasted up in the order in which they are to be printed.

You are responsible for the design and clarity of the product: smudges, typos, and errors of any kind in the copy are your responsibility, not the printer's. Remember: what you see is what you get, so take time to remove smudges, stray lines, and excess rubber cement and to proofread the copy carefully. Be sure the pages are laid out in the correct order.

Avoid using a photocopy, colored paper, and light ink drawings in your original paste-up since these will not reproduce well. Since brown, black, red, and dark blue reproduce the best, use those colors for ink or line drawings. Also note that glossy paper is better for photo reproduction than the less expensive bond paper.

Ask the printer for a blueprint proof. This is the stage just before the final printed copy, and it gives you one last chance to pick up mistakes not discovered earlier. It's also possible that the print shop may have made an error, which you can correct at this stage.

Camera-ready copy may be produced through desktop publishing or typewritten copy that has been laid out and pasted up for reproduction.

You can get more type per page when you have a newsletter typeset than when it is typewritten. A commercial print shop uses a single sheet of paper that is 11-by-17-inches. The sheet is printed then folded in half to an 8½-by-11-inch size. If it is to be mailed, it is usually folded again in thirds to fit a standard number 10 envelope, or sent as a self-mailer.

ALTERNATIVE FUNDING

If your library budget is too small to handle the additional cost of producing a newsletter or brochure, consider alternative sources of funding. Seek money from the PTA, book fairs, Friends of the Library, the community, or any civic group.

Determine in advance a full year's operating costs for the newsletter, including any needed equipment, software, or supplies. Spread the costs out over the year.

There will be major expenditures for printing and mailing. Some costs to include in your estimate are:

* Bulk mail permit
* Envelopes if a self-mailer is not used
* Mailing house charges for affixing labels and stuffing envelopes
* Postage
* Film
* Pencils and pens
* Typewriter ribbons
* Photocopying charges
* Posterboards for preparing a camera-ready master

SCHEDULES

If possible, plan publication and mailing schedules to tie in to special events planned at the school or library. Avoid sending the newsletter before, during, or just after a holiday or when the administration is mailing out information. Develop a month-by-month publications calendar that includes the special events you identified. Plan ahead. Depending on your library, you may decide to suspend publication during the summer months.

CONCLUSION

Once you have determined an annual budget, production method and schedule, move on to the next step in newsletter production: design. Chapter 3 presents design techniques for creating an eye-catching newsletter, flyer, brochure, or pamphlet.

3 ELEMENTS OF DESIGN

"Decisions, decisions, decisions . . ."

FACTORS AFFECTING READABILITY

Black on white

Upper and lower case

Ragged right

Two columns

Bar charts

Good design enhances the readability of the publication, attracts the reader's attention, increases interest in reading the material, and makes the publication easy to recognize.

The following tips will help you create a more readable publication:

- Use black ink on a white background for the text; upper- and lower-case letters; and ragged right columns. Bold-face letters, underlining, and words in all capital letters are less readable.
- Two columns of 40 characters per line, with a half-inch margin between the columns, enhances readability.
- Bar charts are easier to understand then line graphs. If you use bar charts, indicate percentages by using numbers or symbols rather than colors or shades of gray.

NAMEPLATE/LOGO

The first design decision you should make is what your logotype or nameplate will look like and where to position it on the page. The logotype or nameplate usually consists of the name of the newsletter, a design that identifies your school or library, publication date, volume, and issue number. You might also include a phrase describing your newsletter if the name does not do so. Designing the logo and naming the newsletter are two of the most important decisions you will make.

If you have no money, sponsor a contest for library patrons to design the logo. Or you can recruit a graphic artist from among staff, volunteers, or other members of the community. Try to recruit the person to design your nameplate, too.

If you have a little money, your local university or college art departments are an excellent resource for this kind of assistance. They frequently charge less than professional graphic designers.

If you have still more money, hire a professional to design your nameplate and logo.

NAMEPLATE STOCK

Once you decide on the nameplate, you may want to have the print shop print a year's supply of paper with the nameplate on it. This will reduce the overall cost of the newsletter and will ensure the consistency of the paper type and quality for each issue of the volume. The nameplate should identify your library clearly and quickly. A unique, streamlined design will be visually appealing and make it easy for the reader to identify the newsletter.

PAPER

If copies are to be photocopied, an additional color is not a consideration. If they are to be printed, you must decide whether you will use one color only or add a second color. Remember that using multiple colors requires more work on the part of the print shop and so results in higher costs. Also, not all ink colors reproduce well. Ask to see samples of the ink and paper color combinations you are considering before committing yourself to a particular combination.

Some of the more readable combinations are:

- Black ink with yellow paper.
- Green ink with white paper.
- Blue ink with white paper.
- White ink with blue paper.
- Black ink with white paper.

If you decide to use two-color printing, consider using the second color either for the name of the newsletter and the logo, or for only one of those elements. This will enable the print shop to print a year's supply of the nameplate.

Select the color and weight of paper for the newsletter. Sixty-pound white offset stock is usually adequate. It does not have the ink show-through of lighter weight paper, nor does it require the costlier postage of heavier weight paper. Colored papers can be difficult to read. The best choices are cream, ivory, pale gray, pale blue, or pale yellow. Fluorescent, deep, or bright colors are more difficult to read. Look at the swatch books or paper samples available from the print shop to assist you in your selection.

Be sure to ask the print shop for samples of newsletters printed on paper of the color and weight you are considering.

SAMPLE MASTHEAD

LINCOLN DISPATCH

1 Big Sky Road
Starfall, WY
(307) 555-9797

Staff:
Reporter: Melva Dewey
Editor: Bobby Books
Publisher: Lincoln High
School

Deadlines:
Jan. 15   Sept. 15
March 15 Nov. 15
May 15

Published 5 times a year.
Copyright © 1991 Lincoln
Dispatch

Volume 3 Number 1

MASTHEAD

A masthead is a quick and easy way to establish a look of professionalism. It is usually a box with the newsletter's name, address, telephone number; editor's and publisher's names; frequency of publication; copyright notice; and volume (a year's worth of issues) and issue number. Remember: the copyright notice must include the copyright symbol, date, and name of publication. It may be positioned either on the front page or in the masthead. The masthead might also be an appropriate place to include your library's hours, services available, and how to access them. The masthead is normally placed on an inside or back page.

TYPEFACE

Decide which typeface to use, and then use the same typeface throughout the issue. The size of the type can vary; the typeface itself should not, although you can use italic or bold versions of it. Typeface size is measured in points. To insure readability, the smallest size to use is 9 points; the largest is 12 points. The smaller the point size, the smaller the size of the letters and the more copy you can get on a page. All typefaces are either serif or sans serif. A serif is a small line at the top and/or bottom of each letter. Serifs create a visual "hook," which facilitates reading the words. Sans serif typefaces do not have these small lines (see Figure 3-1).

Sans serif is acceptable for headlines, but not for the body of text. If you are using a typewriter, word processor, or desktop publishing software, check your manual to see what typefaces are available for use with your machine or system. Times Roman is the best known serif typeface; Helvetica is a commonly used sans serif typeface.

FIGURE 3-1 Examples of Serif and Sans Serif Faces

Times Roman 14 point (serif).

Helvetica 14 point (sans serif).

Times Roman 18 point bold (serif).

Helvetica 18 point bold (sans serif).

HEADLINES

Decide on the positioning of your headlines. Will they be centered, flush with the left margin, or indented? (Flush with the left margin is often considered easier to read.) Will they be the same size type as the text or larger? (A larger size will attract more attention and break up the page, setting off the beginning of a new article or column.) Will they be in regular or bold type? (Bold will help the reader to identify the beginning of the article.)

Here's an example of a centered headline:

ONLINE CATALOG INSTALLED

We now have an online catalog. It took volunteers two months to put barcode labels on all the library's books.

This is an example of a headline that is flush left:

ONLINE CATALOG INSTALLED

We now have an online catalog. It took volunteers two months to put barcode labels on all the library's books.

PAGE FORMAT

Next, decide on the page format. Use the same format throughout the issue and continue to use it for the entire volume. This will increase the recognizability of your newsletter and help the reader develop familiarity with the arrangement of the material. If you have an 8½-by-11-inch page, then you can have two columns of approximately 3¼ inches each or three columns of 2¼ inches each. The two-column format is the preferred one for a newsletter. More detailed information on page formats is covered in Chapter 10.

BORDERS AND RULES

Decide if you will use borders. Borders are lines around the page, a column, an article, or a photo. How thick will the line be? Will the horizontal lines be wider or narrower than the vertical lines? Will the border be straight, curved, or angular?

Will you use rules? (A rule is a line placed under the headline, before an article, after an article, above or below a photo, or at the beginning or end of a column.) If so, how wide will they be, and when will they be used? It is important to be consistent in your use of rules.

GRAPHICS

Will you use photos or other graphics in your newsletter? If so, how many will you include per issue? What percentage of your newsletter will be devoted to graphics? What kind will you include? Photos, clip art, charts, or graphs? If you intend to use photos, what kind and what size will you use? Photos, clip art, or other graphics can add variety to your newsletter. You can place graphics in one column or spread them across two columns to add interest and to break up a two-column format.

MAILING

If you will be mailing the newsletter, you must allow the top one-third of the last page for mailing information: your library's return address, a nonprofit notice, the mailing label, and any descriptive statement you wish to make.

PAGE NUMBERS

You should number the pages of your newsletter, even if it is only two pages. Decide whether you will number each volume consecutively, or if you will begin with page one with the first issue each year. Consider where you will place the page number. Will it be in the upper right or left corner? Lower right or left corner? Centered at the top or bottom?

FIGURE 3-2   One Possible Layout for Table of Contents

LINCOLN DISPATCH

Vol. 1	June	Issue 5

MAY DAY BOOK FAIR

The May Day Book Fair was a resounding success. The Library was able to gather over 1,700 books and 400 magazines for the sale. Some of them were worn books from our library. Many were donations from parents and other friends of the Lincoln Library.

Sophomore students helped set up the booksale tables and managed to decorate the gym for the May Day festivities, too!

Junior students worked at the sale during the morning and were relieved by Seniors in the afternoon.

After the sale was over, students from all three grades helped clean up the gym.

The sale raised $813.55. The money will be used to buy books, educational videos and a new display board.

Plans are under way to make this an annual fundraising event for the Lincoln Library. Be sure to think of next year's May Day Book Fair whenever you get through reading a paperback or magazine. Just drop any books or magazines you want to donate in the bright yellow carton by the Library check out desk.

A big thanks to all the students, parents and school staff who helped make the May Day Book Fair a success!

CENSORED!

Books which have faced censorship are a varied bunch. See if you can match the book and the objection raised against it for the titles listed below.

_____ 1. **Ordinary People**
_____ 2. **A Light in the Attic**
_____ 3. **Little Red Riding Hood Retold and Illustrated**
_____ 4. **Brave New World**
_____ 5. **Catcher in the Rye**
_____ 6. **Slaughterhouse Five**

A. "violence, promotes drinking"
B. "takes God's name in vain and draws it through the mud"
C. "depiction of the sex act"
D. "filth, smut"
E. "demonic, mocks God"
F. "littered with dirty words"

(Answers: 1C, 2E, 3A, 4D, 5B, 6F)

TABLE OF CONTENTS

Will you include a table of contents box for each issue? It is best to have it on the first page of the newsletter. Where will you position it on the page? Lower right? Across two columns? Alone in a narrower column (if you are using a three column offset format in which two columns are wider than the third)? One possibility is shown in Figure 3-2.

SPACING

Typefaces vary in the amount of space that exists between characters. The amount of vertical spacing between lines of text is called leading (pronounced led-ding). Decide how much space between the characters and lines of text looks most attractive to you. There is no hard-and-fast rule for this since it is dependent on other decisions you have made, such as the number of columns, the style and size of the typeface you are using, the kind of headline decisions you have made, whether or not borders and rules are used, and the placement of any boxes or graphics on the page.

Typewriter type is usually elite, which allows 12 characters to the inch, or pica, which allows 10 characters to the inch. Pica type will have a more open appearance since there are fewer characters per line.

It will be up to you whether or not to have two spaces after periods and whether to double-space lines. Adding extra space at the beginning of a paragraph sets it off. Extra space can also identify the beginning or ending of an article.

These design decisions will determine how much space you will have available for articles. Make these decisions before you begin writing.

GUIDELINES

Simple language

Essential facts

Positive

Brief rules

Good graphics

Color

BROCHURES AND PAMPHLETS

When you design brochures and pamphlets, always include the name of your library, address, phone number, hours of service, services available, and how to access them.

Keep the language simple and straightforward. Give the essential information only.

State the information in positive terms telling your reader what you can do, not what you can't do.

If the brochure or pamphlet gives rules, keep the list short and include only the necessary regulations.

Add graphics when appropriate. They help increase the visual appeal of the brochure, making it more likely that people will pick it up and read it.

Include color when you can, but remember to use ink and paper color combinations that are crisp and readable.

FLYERS

GUIDELINES

Accuracy

Professional lettering

Easy to read

Proofread

There are two basic types of flyers for libraries—those that announce an event and those that give information about a service.

When designing an event flyer, make sure all the information given for the event is correct. Use professional lettering; hand lettering is distracting and decreases readability.

Service flyers are designed to inform, so make sure the instructions are clear and specific. Group instructions into small sections for better comprehension. Test the information for clarity by having someone unfamiliar with the service read it before it is printed. Then remedy any vague or confusing instructions.

Use illustrations where appropriate, and be sure to include a statement urging the reader to ask the staff for further help, if needed.

CONCLUSION

Well-designed materials will capture your reader's attention, increase interest, and make your publications identifiable. The next chapter will provide ways to develop articles, suggest sources for ideas, and describe the kinds of articles you may wish to include in your newsletter.

4 DEVELOPING IDEAS AND SOURCES

"All the news . . ."

Okay, you have figured out the budget for your newsletter and have made the basic design decisions. Now you are ready to start writing, right? No! Before you begin writing, consider what constitutes news for your readers. And remember, you are writing a newsletter.

- What type of articles are you going to include?
- What is your focus?
- Who are your readers?
- What message do you want to send them, and how do you want to send it?

ORGANIZING THE CONTENT

One approach is to structure each issue around a central theme. For example, if you are automating your card catalog, the issue could explain what teachers, students, or other users can expect to encounter during the process. One article could explain the benefits of automation. A second could provide detailed information on what the new catalog screens will look like. A third item could be a sidebar (set-off text containing brief information related to the article) describing how the library will use or sell the old card catalog furniture. A fourth item could be the reminiscences of a student, parent, or teacher about the first time he or she used a card catalog.

REGULAR COLUMNS
You might also add to the article mix a series of regular columns—perhaps a question-and-answer column for recurring reference questions or one providing brief information on new acquisitions.

Although bibliographic citations are a favorite with librarians, carefully consider your readers before including this type of information. Instead, you might provide brief, informative, and entertaining background pieces on the new materials.

FEATURES

Another approach is to begin the newsletter with the same kind of article each issue. You might feature a different library user (perhaps a teacher) in each issue as the lead article. Or highlight various sections or programs of the library. Try to include anecdotes or patrons' comments in articles to provide human interest for topics that might otherwise seem overly technical or specialized.

NEWS STORIES

News stories might include announcements of meetings and programs. Make them more than just calendars of events. Tell your readers who the meeting or program is for, what it is about, and where and why it is being held. Follow up in the next issue with an article reporting on the event itself, including quotations from participants. Remember, the purpose of the newsletter is to provide news in a letter format, so write in a personal, informative style—as though you were talking to your readers.

Letters from teachers, patrons, or staff, book reviews, policy changes, and information about new services are other possible items of interest. Other examples are articles detailing special services such as the availability of audiovisuals.

If possible, do not include a column by the editor. This type of column has done more to turn off readers than any other single item in a newsletter. It gives the impression the newsletter belongs to the editor rather than to the readers.

FINDING IDEAS

SOURCES

Clip file

Ads

Commercials

Dictionary

Encyclopedia

Readers

Questionnaire

The following are suggestions for developing headline, article, and column ideas:

- Develop a file of advertisements. Clip advertisements from magazines, newsletters, and newspapers that capture your attention and use them to help you write catchy headlines.
- Keep copies of well-designed, well-written flyers, brochures, and other printed materials.
- Notice radio or television commercials that engage your interest, amuse you, or have visual appeal.

Write down their memorable phrases and try to modify them for use in your newsletter—perhaps to add interest to the headline of an otherwise routine story.

- Another good source for finding catchy phrases and eyecatching copy is the bulletin of the Advertising Council. It lists the Council's campaigns and the addresses of campaign directors, from whom you can request a copy of the printed materials that complement television spots. For a copy of the bulletin, write to: Public Service Advertising Bulletin, The Advertising Council, Inc., 825 Third Ave., New York, NY 10022.
- Indispensable sources are a dictionary, almanac, encyclopedia, *Statistical Abstracts*, and other general reference books. They enable you to check facts and can provide you with ideas for brief items (known as fillers) to use when you have limited space.
- Your readers are also a source of material. Talk to them. Find out what they are interested in and write an article to fill the need.
- Questionnaires can also be a source. Survey a group of library patrons and write an article based on the findings.

Contests can generate interest. Why not hold a contest to name a column, or a library program?

Quizzes are an excellent way to capture attention and teach at the same time. A true-or-false questionnaire, for example, can correct misinformation. An example of a newsletter quiz is shown in Figure 3–2.

CONCLUSION

With creativity and work, you can develop an endless supply of ideas and sources for newsletter articles.

The next chapter provides guidelines for expressing those ideas in professionally crafted writing.

5 WRITING TIPS

"Say it with words . . ."

A newsletter should be quick and easy to read. Too often newsletters are written as if they were scaled-down versions of newspapers or magazines. They are not; they are letters to your readers. Keeping that in mind, use the following guidelines to create a well-written newsletter.

STYLE TIPS

Be brief

Be simple

Be clear

Indent often

Use the word "You"

WORK TOWARD READABILITY

SIMPLICITY
Keeping it simple will increase the readability of your writing. Use short sentences and be succinct. Limit the number of words with more than two syllables. Have fewer than 16 words in a sentence wherever possible. If a sentence is over 25 words, break it into two or more sentences.

Keep the sentence structure simple. Avoid semicolons. Instead, create two sentences. Drop unnecessary introductory phrases. Keep prepositions to a minimum. Overuse of the words across, against, among, before, behind, beside, between, by, despite, for, in, into, off, on, onto, out, toward, up, under, and without adds little information to the sentence and can create needlessly complex sentences. For example, instead of

> Marty skied between the trees without hurting himself despite the many branches jutting from the tree trunks.

Use

> Marty skied between the trees.

Write simple declarative sentences free of complex clauses or compound thoughts. Use simple, concrete terms and direct statements. Avoid stiff, formal phrases.

Use contractions. Although formal writing discourages

their use, they personalize the newsletter. If the contraction sounds right when read aloud, use it. Also, the word "you" gives your writing a personal feel.

Indent paragraphs; they are easier to read than block style.

The more difficult the topic, the simpler your writing should be.

STYLE TIPS

Be precise

Don't repeat yourself

BREVITY

The limited space available in a newsletter requires brevity. Get the essential information to your reader concisely. Make the main idea of the article the first sentence. Avoid beginning with an explanatory background paragraph. When possible, use lists to make detailed information easier to understand.

Think of your writing in terms of a series of telegrams, not essays. The longer the piece, the less likely it is to be read.

Make each word in a sentence meaningful and avoid redundancy. Instead of

The meeting will be at 3 p.m. in the afternoon.

Use

The meeting will be at 3 p.m.

Try to write precisely and to the point.

STYLE TIPS

Be accurate

Use active verbs

Be logical

CLARITY

To achieve clarity, choose your words carefully. Avoid library jargon. Select words that are familiar, easy to understand, and expressive.

Check your spelling. Misusing or misspelling words confuses the reader and damages your credibility.

Check your facts. Readers often make decisions based on the information you give them.

Use strong nouns and verbs. Write in the active, not passive, voice. Use the present, rather than past, tense.

Limit the use of adjectives and adverbs. Avoid metaphors.

Put the complete article on one page when possible, since continuing a story on another page breaks the reader's concentration and lessens interest.

Do not have subjects and predicates too widely separated. Instead of

The PTA is donating materials for the development of a special collection on literacy.

Use

The PTA is donating literacy materials.

Place verbs early in the sentence. Instead of

In light of a restrictive budget, the library will not be able to purchase an online catalog system this year.

Use

The library lacks the funds to buy an online catalog system.

Make every sentence add to or explain what you say in your first sentence (which should be the topic sentence).

The library has a new online catalog. It will replace the old card catalog and make it easier to inventory the collection. Next Wednesday, Samantha Kiest will demonstrate how to use it.

Put the article's main points in one of the following sequences:

- Chronological
- Most important to least important
- What action was taken and its results
- Broad statements to specific ones
- Pros and cons.

Present ideas in a logical order. Imagine that you are the reader. Ask yourself how the sentence, paragraph, and article sound from the reader's point of view.

STYLE TIPS

Use action verbs

Be upbeat

Use subheads

Use logical line breaks

Use fresh words

Use short words

Use larger type

HEADLINES
Good headlines enhance a newsletter's readability. The following techniques will enable you to write effective headlines:

- Use both a subject and a verb in the headline. Use action verbs and short words whenever possible. Make the headline upbeat, interesting, or catchy.
- Use headings to highlight important points. Use subheads to break up longer articles.

- Avoid trite or overused words.
- Avoid using acronyms or initials in a headline since they can confuse the reader.
- Make sure you break the headline at a logical point if it takes more than one line.
- Make the headline larger than other text to indicate clearly where to start reading.

HOW TO WRITE BETTER

Learn about your topic before you begin an article. Make a three- to five-point outline stating the purpose, focus, and intent of the article. Be specific. For example, instead of labeling point one "introduction," state the problem or slant of the topic you are addressing. This technique enables you to clarify what you want to say. If you aren't clear, how can your writing be clear?

BASIC STEPS

The basic steps in writing are:

1. Draft
2. Revise
3. Type
4. Edit
5. Proofread

Then edit and proofread again. You can skip step three if you are using a word processor. If possible, have someone unfamiliar with the substance of the article read it. If this person can't understand it, it needs more work.

PACE YOURSELF

Be kind to yourself when you are writing. Everyone has a different pace. Find yours. Take frequent breaks. One every 15 or 20 minutes works well for many people. Experiment until you discover your pace and how long you can write without losing concentration. Writing is a skill and, like any skill, requires practice. Set reasonable deadlines and start early to finish on time.

Before beginning to write, make sure you know your subject matter and have an article outline prepared. Also make sure you have all the materials you need before you start writing. Finally, reward yourself. When you finish an article, column, issue, or section of an issue, give yourself a treat. This will reinforce your feeling of accomplishment in completing the task.

ANALYZE MISTAKES

One way to cut down on the time and work involved in writing is to analyze your writing mistakes. Learn why and how you are making them, and then correct them. If you don't perform this analysis, you may find yourself making the same mistake over and over.

SOURCES OF HELP

Grammar Hotline

Writer's Digest

Writer magazine

GRAMMAR

Grammar is a nightmare for many people. There are various excellent sources to turn to for help with grammar questions. Hodges' *Harbrace College Handbook* is one. Check the school library, the public library, or a local bookstore for others. Call the English department of your local college or university for recommendations. Or call a grammar hotline for immediate help.

A copy of the *Grammar Hotline Directory*, which gives the names and phone numbers of hotlines in the United States, is included in Appendix E. To obtain an updated copy send a stamped, self-addressed business-letter-sized envelope to: *Grammar Hotline Directory*, Tidewater Community College Writing Center, 1700 College Crescent, Virginia Beach, VA 23456.

Try *Writer's Digest* or *Writer* magazine for suggestions and for lists like "the ten top grammar errors" or "the only two grammar rules you need to know." Add them to your idea file.

To get you started, here is a list of the three most misused word groups:

1. Your and you're. "You're" is used for you are. "Your" indicates ownership:

   Your classroom is on the left.
   You're going to have 23 students for this class.

2. Its and it's. "Its" is possessive. Only use "it's" when you mean "it is":

> Its walls are pale yellow.
> It's homecoming weekend at Dermott High.

3. Their, there, and they're. "Their" is possessive. "There" refers to location. "They're" is the contraction for they are:

> Their bus was late.
> There is the bus.
> They're waiting for the bus.

Don't let fear of making an error stop you from writing a newsletter.

DON'T MENTION IT

Race

Gender

Age

Handicaps

STEREOTYPES
To keep stereotypes and biases out of your writing, avoid stating the following characteristics unless relevant to the story: race, gender, handicap, and age—including a term for an age category such as teenager or senior citizen.

GENERAL RULES

Here are some underlying principles to guide your writing:

- Don't try to impress your readers. Give them the information simply and clearly.
- Don't try to hide anything. If a service is being discontinued, state so directly and give the reason for the change.
- Stress the ways in which people can use the library's equipment, materials, programs, and services. Give examples, with names of teachers or others who have used the material or service. This relates the library to patrons' work or needs. It makes the library more people oriented and, therefore, more interesting to your readers.
- Create an awareness of your library's mission. When writing about specific events, comment on their connection to the library's general goals.

KNOW YOUR AUDIENCE

In addition to mastering writing techniques, you must know your audience and your subject. To write a persuasive article, find out your readers' current views on the topic. To increase their knowledge, learn how much they already know. To change the way your readers do something, find out why they do it the way they do. To get action, discover what motivates your readers.

CONCLUSION

Good newsletter writing depends on simplicity, brevity, and clarity. Know your audience, know your subject, and check your facts. Chapter 6 discusses the next step: to edit and proofread what you have written.

6 EDITING AND PROOFING

"Slash and cut ..."

You've done your research, written the newsletter, typed it, read it from the reader's point of view, and revised it. Now you are ready to proofread it before reproducing it and going public with it. It is best to have someone else proof it with you. If you must do it by yourself, make sure you do the proofing sometime after you've done the writing and revising. Let it sit for a day or two. Otherwise, your eyes may pass right over a misspelled word, an incorrect date, or incorrect names of people or places. You might not notice that the percentages on your chart or graph don't add up or that a number is transposed.

Start writing early so you can lay your manuscript aside and come back to it in a day or two when you are fresh, then proof it.

PROBLEM SPOTS

First line

First paragraph

First page

Top of line

Headlines

Subheads

Titles

PROOFREADING TIPS

Errors seem more noticeable in some areas of a publication than in others. Pay special attention to these problem spots (shown at left) when proofreading.

A sample of standard proofreader's marks is included in the appendix. Keep a copy in your newsletter folder and refer to it as needed.

EDITING

The next step, editing, is related to revising and proofreading, yet is different from both of those activities. There are three basic types of editing, each one of which requires a particular approach. The three basic types of editing are: concept editing, line editing, and copy editing.

You will find yourself doing all three.

Concept editing: Concept editing is fun. This is where you let your creativity loose. Read each item of the newsletter separately and decide how you can make it better. Would it be more interesting if the third sentence of a story were first or last? Have you put the topic sentence as the first sentence—not buried in it in the text? Can you liven up the item by changing a word or two? Maybe an entire paragraph should be moved to another place in the article. Move it. Is it really necessary to include the make and model of the new fax machine? If not, delete it. Enjoy yourself during concept editing.

Line editing: Line editing is more detailed. Here you are reading carefully to gauge the cadence of each sentence and the relevancy of each word, sentence, and paragraph. Which word best describes the action, object, concept, or person? Is this word too obscure? Will the readers understand the term "serials acquisition," or would "a new magazine subscription" be a better choice? Is that sentence relevant, or does it slow the reader down without adding to the story? Line editing requires more concentration than concept editing but less than copy editing.

Copy editing: Copy editing is what most people envision when they think of editing. Copy editing is exacting. The copy editor is the one who spots errors in facts, grammar, style, and spelling. This person makes sure the copy is legible, the pages are properly marked, and any instructions for the printer are included. Copy editors need a good dictionary, style manual, grammar book, almanac, and encyclopedia, as well as a copy of the original material used if information was abstracted from another source. If possible, have a staff member known as a stickler for correct grammar act as your copy editor. Select the dictionary, grammar book, and style manual you want the copy editor to use.

CONCLUSION

If you must do it all yourself, leave time between concept editing, line editing, and copy editing. This is the way to do the job well.

Proofreading is easier if you can use a computer software package that checks spelling for you. There are also programs available that point out grammatical errors. The final arbiter, though, is the copy editor.

Chapter 7 describes how to use desktop publishing to create your newsletter.

7 DESKTOP PUBLISHING

"Me and my computer . . ."

Desktop publishing is using a personal computer, software, and printer to produce publications such as newsletters, flyers, handouts, or brochures.

There are a number of advantages associated with using desktop publishing:

ADVANTAGES

Flexibility

Cost savings

Time savings

- You can produce high-quality, professional looking publications without being a professional designer, typesetter, graphic artist, or paste-up specialist, thereby saving time and money.
- You have the flexibility to compose the text, lay out the page, merge text and graphics, and produce camera-ready copy for printing. Seeing the page layout on the screen allows you to make changes quickly. The original can be photocopied, or copies can be printed by a service bureau.
- You can create a publication that speaks to both sides of the brain. The left side of the brain processes language; the right, visual information. With desktop publishing you can easily blend text and graphics.

DISADVANTAGES

High cost of equipment

Long learning process

Potential for bad design

There are disadvantages, too. The cost may be prohibitive for the beginner who must purchase both equipment and software. It takes time to become familiar with the equipment and software, and time must be factored in as part of the costs.

In addition, simply possessing a desktop publishing system does not endow one with good design sense. It may only make it easier to create poorly designed publications.

Desktop publishing is exciting and rewarding. It offers nearly unlimited possibilities, allows creativity, and produces a feeling of accomplishment once you've used it to produce a publication. But it can bewilder the uninitiated since there is much to learn.

EQUIPMENT DECISIONS

You will be deciding which of the following items to purchase:

- Computer type
- Speed
- Disk
- Surge Protector
- Software
- Monitor
- Printer
- Memory
- Mouse

HARDWARE: WHICH COMPUTER? WHICH ACCESSORIES?

The first decision to make is which computer system to use: IBM (or IBM-compatible) or Macintosh.

If you decide on an IBM or IBM clone, get at least an AT-compatible system. It is an AT if it has the number "286" or higher in its name. The higher the number, the more powerful the computer.

The Macintosh has a Motorola microprocessor and requires a "mouse" to operate. Most models are more expensive than the IBM or IBM clones. Some people believe the Macintosh is easier to use than the IBM. Go to a computer store and try out both to find out which one you are most comfortable using.

Speed: The speed at which your system runs is also important. The higher the number, the faster it runs. Much of the desktop publishing software you will consider buying runs best at 12 megahertz or higher.

Disk: The larger the storage capacity of your hard disk, the better. A hard disk and an external floppy drive is best. Depending on the software you choose, this can be either a $3\frac{1}{2}$-inch or $5\frac{1}{4}$-inch high-density floppy drive. Software packages include floppy disks that you use to install the program on your computer. Some software packages will have a disk of only one size, either $5\frac{1}{4}$-inch or $3\frac{1}{2}$-inch. Be sure you know what the software requires before you decide on the floppy drive size. If your computer system has both floppy drive sizes, you can use various software packages.

Memory: The system memory, or RAM (Random Access Memory), should be at least one megabyte. More memory is better if you can afford it. The higher the RAM number, the more memory your system has. This is where your desktop publishing program is loaded when you are using it; some programs require a large amount of memory to operate.

Mouse: Some software packages require a mouse. The mouse is an accessory approximately the size of a yo-yo. It is connected to the computer with a cable. Rolling the mouse on the surface of the desk moves the cursor around the screen without using the keys. The higher the quality, the more easily maneuvered and long lasting the mouse will be.

Monitor: A VGA monitor with a graphics card is preferable. Decide if you need a color monitor or monochrome (black and white). If you plan to have a paint software program, you will need a color monitor.

Surge Protector: Since a power surge can cause data to be lost or damaged, buy a good surge protector. Do not plug appliances into your computer system's surge protector. Plugging a portable fan or heater, for example, into the surge protector will pull electrical current at uneven levels and cause power surges that may destroy data over a period of time.

Printer: Buying a printer is the next decision. You may decide to use a printing service bureau instead. Some can take your floppy disk and print out the newsletter, flyer, handout, or brochure on a laser printer. This has advantages and drawbacks.

An advantage is that you can put off buying a printer or buy an inexpensive dot-matrix printer for your preliminary work and use the service bureau to print the final camera-ready copy.

One disadvantage is that, since you can't see how the printed copy will look beforehand, you may find that the spacing is off. Because there is usually some difference in spacing between printers, you may be satisfied with the appearance of the page on the monitor, only to find that it looks different once the service bureau prints it.

If there isn't a service bureau that can take your disk and print it, make every effort to buy a laser printer. Get one that will produce copy good enough to use as a camera-ready copy. The Hewlett Packard LaserJet IIP or III fill the bill for IBM (or IBM clone) users. The ImageWriter, LaserMAX, and the LaserWriter 11SC can be used with Macintosh computers. Check with microcomputer manufacturers on the availability of educational discounts. You may save as much as 45 to 50% on the cost of a microcomputer or printer.

SOFTWARE
Next, decide which desktop publishing software fits your needs. There are a number of choices: word processing, page layout, font, paint, and drawing software packages.

Word processing: Word processing software allows you to compose and edit text. You can draw boxes and import graphic files; some have limited page layout capabilities. WordPerfect, PFS: Write, and Wordstar are a few possibilities for IBM users. Microsoft Word and WriteNow complement the Macintosh.

Page layout programs: Page layout programs are used to arrange text into a format. The Xerox Ventura Publisher and Aldus PageMaker are two rather expensive page layout programs. Start out with a lower-priced package if you are inexperienced. Popular ones are PFS:First Publisher, Springboard Publisher, GEM Desktop Publisher, and Publish It!.

A word processing program may be all you need. Some can import files, edit text, position graphics, format text in multiple columns, and perform other layout functions.

Buy a word processing program, use it for a while, then decide if a page layout program is necessary. If you work with the program for a few weeks before taking a training class on it, the class will be more meaningful.

Fonts: There are numerous font programs available. Fontsy (for the IBM) and Fontographer and Adobe Type Manager (for the Macintosh) are just a few.

Your word processing software will have some fonts available, as will your laser printer. If you buy additional fonts, check the software box to see if they will work with your printer.

Build families of typefaces if you decide to buy more fonts. For example, if you have Times Roman 6, 8, 10, and 12 point fonts with normal, bold, and italic options, buy a package with

---

FIGURE 7-1   A Family of Type Can Be Lightface, Boldface, and Italic In Various Sizes

Times Roman 14 point normal.

Times Roman 14 point italic.

Times Roman 14 point bold.

Times Roman 18 point bold.

Times Roman 24 point bold.

Times Roman 30 point bold.

Times Roman 14, 18, 24, and 30 point normal and bold fonts. See Figure 7-1.

Keep in mind the personality you want to give your publication when you select typefaces. Typefaces can give a formal, casual, modern, or traditional feel to your publication. Look at what's available, and decide which ones best express the mood you want to establish for your library. Remember: the tone of your writing and design create an image for your library. They define the atmosphere the reader will expect to find there.

KEEP IN MIND

Less is better

Be consistent

Keep line spacing in proportion

DESIGN

Regardless of which typeface you select, strive to produce a clean design. The following tips will help:

- Less is better. Use no more than three sizes of type. Don't crowd the page with a variety of types and sizes.

- Achieve consistency by using one size and style of type for headlines. Use another for text. Make it easy for your readers to recognize which size and style of type indicates which kind of information. Put the most important information in the largest type, the least important in the smaller type, and everything else in the medium type.
- Line spacing refers to the amount of space from the bottom of one line of type to the top of the next line of type. This is particularly important in headlines. Too much line spacing in a headline reduces its impact. Keep line spacing proportionate, and don't add it just to fill up a column.
- Don't justify large type in a headline to the left and right margins, since too much space between the letters slows down reading. Set a headline flush left or center it.
- It's possible to create a gray or patterned background, then type over the background. But be careful—letters can blend into the background when printed with a laser printer.

PAINT AND DRAW

Paint and draw programs enable you to create your own graphics. A paint program allows you to fill in areas to intensify the image. You can also lighten an image by deleting some of the dots of which it is composed. As its name implies, a draw program enables you to draw an image.

You can buy clip art software programs. These pre-drawn images are similar to traditional paper clip art illustrations. You import the image you want into your word processing or page layout program, then position it on the page.

PC Paintbrush and Colorix VGA Paint are examples of paint programs. Arts & Letters, Corel Draw, Micrografx Draw Plus, and Harvard Draw Partner are a few of the draw programs available. Two for Macintosh users are the Adobe Illustrator and the Aldus FreeHand.

SCANNERS

Do you have a photo or illustration you want to include in your publication? A scanner allows you to copy the image into your document and manipulate it.

There are two types of scanners: optical character scanners and image scanners. Optical character scanners are used to translate typed manuscript into copy that is stored in your system. Image scanners are used to digitize graphics such as logos, line art, illustrations, and photographs.

The scanner converts the hard copy image into an array of dots. The dots can be black, white, or shades of gray. The software used with the scanner then takes the dot patterns and compares them to stored letters. The software inserts the correct character when a match is found. It inserts a special character when it is unable to find a match. The accuracy rate for most scanned text is 95% (or less), which means you will have to edit at least five percent of the text.

There are handheld, flatbed, or sheetfed scanners. If the operator's hand shakes using a handheld scanner, a poorer scanned image may result. A flatbed scanner holds a sheet stable and scans it. A sheetfed scanner automatically feeds the sheets through the scanner.

Scanners require a large amount of memory to work, and scanned images require a lot of memory space. Storing one eight-bit gray-scale halftone image can easily take more than a full megabyte of disk space. Also, it takes a relatively long time to print gray-scale scanned images.

The prices of scanners vary depending on the quality and options selected. If you would need a scanner only rarely, consider using a service bureau instead. Commercial print shops often provide scanning service.

Scanners recognize some typefaces better than others. It's a good idea to have the service bureau do a test of the item to be scanned so you can get an idea of what to expect. Remember that you will have to insert the missing characters yourself after the text is scanned.

PURCHASING EQUIPMENT

HARDWARE BUYING TIPS

Newsletters, brochures, flyers, and pamphlets can be produced using equipment the library has. However, you may want to upgrade or replace existing equipment to achieve a higher quality result or to make your job easier. If you are responsible for choosing and purchasing the equipment, consider your local area dealers.

Many libraries make purchases from local vendors when possible since the vendors' taxes support the system. It builds good will, and local retailers often offer discounts to libraries. This may outweigh a reduced purchase price from a store far from home. It is also advisable to make purchases locally to take advantage of start-up and ongoing assistance.

Although not generally recommended for libraries, ordering hardware and software by mail is an alternative to a computer store.

There are certain potential problems to be aware of if you order by mail.

1. Check the shipping charges. Know what you are agreeing to and have a record of the agreed terms. Include a letter with your order, specifying such terms as the time of delivery and warranty agreements. Make sure you understand the warranty terms. Is the product under warranty by the dealer or by the factory? If it is under dealer warranty, find out if all the system components are under one warranty or if each component is under a separate warranty.

2. Money-back guarantees may not really mean that you will get your money back. If you return the item, some companies charge a restocking fee, which can run as high as 15% of the item's cost.

3. Check for disclaimers. Some companies do not allow returns of non-defective items. For example, if you discover that a system you ordered does not work with your power supply, you might not be able to return it.

4. Check the product as soon as it arrives to make certain it works properly, while it is still under guarantee.

5. When you buy a hard drive by mail, find out if it is a new hard drive or a factory refurbished unit. Repaired ones are more likely to crash.

6. Ask other librarians about the reliability and effectiveness of the computer systems they are using. Also inquire about the reliability of the dealer from whom they made the purchase.

SOFTWARE BUYING TIPS

Make sure the warranty card is in the package. Without it, you will not be able to get help from the user support de-

partment and will not be offered program upgrades at a reduced price.

Check to see if the word processing software comes with
mail merge, spell check, and thesaurus features.

Check the desktop publishing package for extra fonts, tem-
plates, and printer drive utilities.

Be sure to specify the version of the software you expect to
receive. As a program is improved, a higher number is as-
signed to it. You will want the latest version.

Install and test the software on your computer as soon as
you get it. Make sure it works with your printer and that you
can save and retrieve data.

CONCLUSION

Desktop publishing provides a multitude of options that allow
you to produce your own publication without the aid of a designer, typesetter, graphic artist, or paste up specialist. It
does, however, require certain equipment and software. If you
don't have these available—or have the funds to buy what
you need—you can still produce an attractive publication.
The next chapter tells you how.

8 OTHER PRODUCTION METHODS

"Compose yourself..."

Desktop publishing is only one way to compose your publication. Three other popular methods are: typewriter, word processor, or typesetting.

Although a typewriter will enable you to produce newsletters, brochures, pamphlets, and flyers, your job will be much easier with a word processor. Most librarians have access to a computer with word-processing capabilities. This allows you to save and easily edit the text. The difficult task is in designing the first newsletter. Once that is done, you can fill in the shell each time with new information.

Typesetting produces a quality product. You give the copy to the printer for typesetting rather than making a camera-ready copy first.

The production steps differ for each method, as explained below.

TYPEWRITER COMPOSITION

Typewriter composition is the easiest of the four methods. Use an electric typewriter if possible, since the weight of the keystrokes is even, resulting in an even type weight. A typewriter with a correction feature will make it easier to type a clean copy.

The first step in typewriter composition is to create an original manuscript by typing the articles.

For clear characters use a new carbon ribbon and clean the keys before you begin. Use a clean sheet of smooth white paper.

If you don't have a typewriter with a correction feature, use correction fluid to fix one or two letters, typing the correct letters over the dried fluid. To correct a line of type, cover the line with self-adhesive correction tape and retype the line.

You can decide on the general format for the newsletter and type articles to fit the format, or you can type each article on a separate sheet of paper in column format, then cut out each item and paste them up in the order you want.

"Typing to fit" means you type the article to fit the length and width of the column you have. First, decide if you want a full-measure (one column all the way across the page), two-column, or three-column newsletter.

If you choose a full-measure column, decide on the average line length you want—seven inches, for example. Look at the scale on your typewriter. It will show that seven inches equals about 84 characters or spaces. Set left and right margin guides for 84 characters and start composing your stories in that length.

> Elite: 1 inch = 12 characters
>
> Pica: 1 inch = 10 characters

You can also determine the number of characters in a line by using a typewriter gauge. A typewriter line gauge looks like a ruler. Typewriter type is usually elite (12 characters to the inch) or pica (ten characters to the inch). The typewriter gauge has the number of picas per inch on one edge and the characters per inch for elite type on the other.

Figure out how many lines of type you have on the first page and on inside pages to see how many total lines of type are available for your articles.

For example, the front page may be 45 lines long and the inside page, 58 lines. Note the number of lines for each item, adding space between stories. Next decide on the order of the stories. Note the number of lines for each one, adding one line for each space between stories. You can thus determine if all the articles will fit.

Here's an example of how you might use the line count method for a page with 45 lines: The first article is 25 lines long. There is one line of space between the first and second article. The second article is 19 lines long. 25 + 1 + 19 = 45. You now know that you have enough room on the page for both articles plus one line of space between the articles.

You can follow the same procedure for a two-column format. The two-column format is more versatile in terms of photo and graphic layout. Long lines of type are hard to read. Keep the lines short so the reader's eyes do not tire and reread lines. Forty to 45 characters per line is a good general rule to follow regardless of the type size you use.

If you are considering a three-column format, you may find that this design works best with the typeset method, where the right-hand margins can be justified.

Another consideration is the size of the typewriter type used. The size of type is measured in points. One point equals $\frac{1}{72}$ of an inch. Twelve points equals one pica.

This is an example of 10 point type.

This is an example of 12 point type.

If you have an interchangeable typewriter element machine, you can change typeface sizes or styles as needed by changing elements. For example, you could use Courier 10-point type for the body text in the newsletter and 14-point type for headlines.

You can also use press-on letters for headlines, as shown in Figure 8-1.

The spacing between characters has an impact on the readability and appearance of the newsletter. Pitch is the term used to describe the spacing between characters. A 12-pitch type element has 12 characters to the inch; a 10-pitch type element has 10 characters to the inch. The 10-pitch type element gives a more open look to the newsletter since there is more space between the individual letters.

Check with your typewriter supplier to find out what size and style of typefaces are available.

After typing all the articles, cut them out and do a rough layout and paste-up. To do this, lay the articles out in the desired arrangement, page by page. Next, attach them with masking tape to the paper. Then lay in photocopies of art, graphs, photos, and any other graphics. After determining where to place each article and graphic, proofread the text and note any corrections or changes. If you need to correct a typographical error, indicate the typo in the margin with a non-reproducing blue pencil. The next step is to type the final copy, do the final layout, and paste up, leaving spaces for inserting artwork. Attach the art, graphs, photos, and any other graphics. You now have a master—camera-ready copy—that you can mimeograph or photocopy.

If you plan to have your newsletter typeset, you won't need to have camera-ready copy. Just give your copy to the printer, who will typeset it. You will have to decide on the type size and amount of space you want between lines. Select some sample typefaces and take them with you to the printers.

FIGURE 8-1   Press-on Letters May Be Used For Headlines

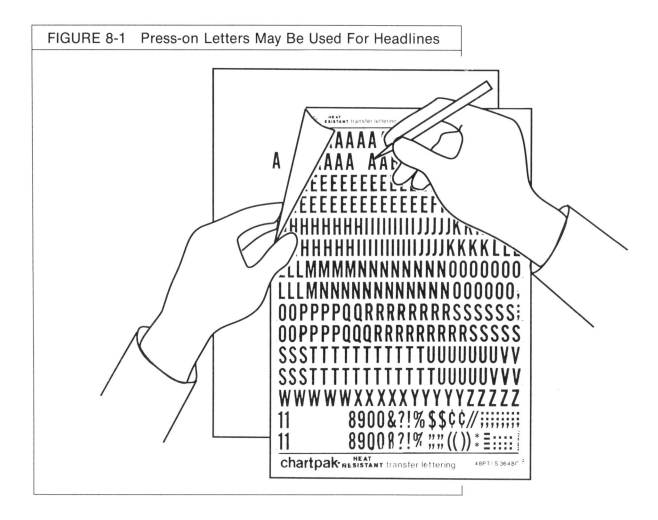

Marking up copy for typesetting is called specifying type or writing type specs. Type specs tell your typesetter what you want. Provide the following information to your type-setter:

1. Name of the typeface(s) to be used.
2. The type size to use for body type and headlines.
3. The amount of line spacing you want between lines and stories.
4. The column width.
5. Whether the lines are to be:
   a. Justified (J) means the right and left hand mar-gins will be even.
   b. Flush left, ragged right (FL/RR) means the left hand margin will be even and the right will be uneven.

     c. Ragged left, flush right (RL/FR) means the left hand margin will be uneven and the right hand margin will be even.

     d. Centered (C) means the lines will be centered between the margins.

  6. Paragraph treatment:

     a. Indented (how many spaces).

     b. Flush (even with the left margin).

WORD PROCESSOR COMPOSITION

First, create an original manuscript by keyboarding the articles. Then edit, format, proofread, and do a rough layout using the word processor screen instead of hard copy. Store the articles and format in the computer. Print out a hard copy draft on a printer. Make a copy of any artwork or other graphics and place them where you want them on the page.

Make any changes needed and do final layout and paste up. Use the finished master for reproduction. Keep in mind how to arrange the pages on the sheet so they will be printed in the correct order.

The word processor is a step between typewriters and computers.

TYPESET COMPOSITION

Create the original manuscript using a typewriter, word processor, or desktop publishing. Take the original to a commercial printer, who will prepare it for typesetting. It will be scanned, keyboarded, or electronically transmitted (depending on which kind of original you provided) to the typeset machine.

Typesetting—turning typed copy into lines of printed text—is the most expensive method of composition. It is also the most time-consuming, so allow extra time in your production schedule.

Individual characters used to be cast into metal, called hot type. In a process called letterpress, the characters were locked into forms, then ink was added and the lines of words were printed on sheets of paper.

Most composition equipment now is electronic photo typesetting or digital typesetting. Some equipment can scan or digitize the original manuscript or read the formatting codes from a floppy disk.

After the type has been set, the printer will give you galleys or proofs, which you check for errors. Make any corrections necessary and return the galleys to the printer. If the mistake was due to your error, you will have to pay for the changes. If it was the printer's fault, you will not have to pay for the correction. After you have approved the galleys, a camera-ready copy will be made.

DESKTOP COMPOSITION

The original manuscript is created using the computer and desktop publishing software. You edit, format, proofread, merge text and graphics, and execute your layout on the monitor screen. The document you produce is stored in a computer file. Then you print out a hard-copy draft for final corrections and check the layout. The original is taken to a commercial printer either on a floppy disk or as hard copy. You may provide a camera-ready copy or have the printer create it.

PASTING UP PAGES

Camera-ready copy means that the pages are ready for the printer to shoot with a photo offset camera. Each page must be laid out and pasted up exactly as it is to appear when printed. The correct order of the finished newsletter pages depends on your awareness of the correct order for paste up.

For example, if you plan to have a four-page newsletter printed on 11-by-17-inch paper folded in half to an $8\frac{1}{2}$-by-11-inch size, you must paste the pages up in the following way:

Back left	Back right
	Page 1

Page 1 on the back right side of the 11-by-17-inch sheet of paper.

Front left	Front right
Page 2	Page 3

Page 2 on the front left side of the 11-by-17-inch sheet of paper. Page 3 on the front right side of the 11-by-17-inch sheet of paper.

Back left	Back right
Page 4	Page 1

Page 4 on the back left side of the 11-by-17-inch sheet of paper.

Once a camera-ready copy is produced, the following production steps occur.

Whatever is to be printed is photographed, and plates are made from the negatives. The negatives are put on a press, and ink is added. The press produces the image of the plate on paper. Then the press operator runs off several press sheets to check the color and intensity of the ink. Once any needed adjustments are made, the press run is completed. The plates are attached to the press and printed. The press sheets are trimmed, and folded in half if it is an 11-by-17-inch sheet to be folded to 8½-by-11-inches.

If more than one 11-by-17-inch sheet is needed, the newsletter is assembled by inserting one sheet into the other.

The newsletter is folded again if you specified a second fold such as a half-page or letterfold.

If the newsletter is to be a self-mailer, labels are attached. If it is to be mailed in an envelope, each copy is inserted into an envelope and labels are affixed. The envelopes are sorted by zipcode, and postage is affixed if required. The envelopes are bundled and delivered to the post office.

9 GRAPHICS

"A picture is worth . . ."

You can use graphics to highlight or simplify information, to build ideas, make comparisons, or show relationships. Thought, planning, taste, and a little extra effort are required to achieve well-designed graphics.

Choose the best graphic form for your audience and the message you are trying to convey. Are you showing your reader how to do something? If so, a line drawing, illustration, or photo may be the best choice. Are you trying to show an increase in circulation? A chart can effectively convey the message. Are you trying to introduce your reader to a new staff member? Use a photo of the person.

Consider the quality of the graphic. Amateurish drawings diminish a professional image and are best left out of your publication.

GOOD GRAPHICS SHOULD BE:

Accurate

Limited to the best items

Consistent in style

SELECTING GRAPHICS

Keep these tips in mind for selecting graphics:

- Accurate information is more important than a cute or clever graphic.
- Use a minimum of graphic elements. Too many can detract from your message or distract your reader. Avoid adding graphics simply because you have them.
- Use the same color background throughout the publication for a consistent image, and use traditional color symbolism: red for danger, yellow for warmth, green for growth. Gray projects a formal image; blue gives an intellectual, detached feeling.
- Choose a format for presenting graphics and use it consistently. For example, always put a box around an image, or always run it with a caption.

SOURCES

Anthologies

Clip art

Magazines

Other newsletters

Line drawings

GRAPHICS

Sources of ideas for graphics include anthologies of award-winning images. Commercially produced clip-art kits or software packages provide pre-drawn graphics and illustrations. Magazines can be used for borders, typefaces or cartouches, isolations or optical illusions. Cartouches are small ornamental frames within which you can put your own words. Isolations are letters or pictures of which you use only a portion. A picture buried within a larger picture is an example of an isolation.

Keep a file of sample newsletters from which you can extract typeface and design ideas.

Line drawings are also good items for your graphics file. Printing them in black ink on white paper is the best combination for clarity. Other dark colors that reproduce well are brown, red, and dark blue. Avoid using drawings with extensive light shading or those made with light solid lines.

SOURCES

Software

Letter sheets

Publications

LETTERING

Sources for lettering include software programs and dry, pressure-sensitive transfer lettering sheets. Lettering sheets, available at graphic and office supply companies, come in many styles which are useful for expressing the image you want to present of your library. The "transferability" of the letters deteriorates over time, so buy only the quantity you need for a short period. A good rule of thumb is to buy as much as you will use in a month.

You can also use words that you cut from magazines, newspapers, catalogs, and newsletters.

PROS

Increase readability

Project positive image

CONS

Time consuming

Expensive

Difficult to find

PHOTOS

Whether or not to use photos will depend on your audience, message, schedule, and budget. Photos usually increase readership. They can communicate your message more quickly and completely than words alone. They can promote positive public relations. People like to see pictures of themselves in a publication.

On the other hand, it takes time to get a good photo, to decide which photo best conveys your message and is appropriate for your article and publication. Once selected, the photo must be cropped and sized. A caption must be written and a credit line prepared. Photos increase the amount of time it takes to make a rough layout and prepare the final paste-up. They also add to the time the print shop requires to print your publication.

Photos cost money. You have to buy the film and pay for the developing and printing. If you decide to use a photographer, your costs increase. The print shop will charge extra for each photo, too.

Good photos are difficult to find. Some may be inappropriate for the format or subject matter. An inappropriate photo can detract from your message and the image of your publication.

Not all newsletters are appropriate vehicles for photos. If yours isn't, don't use photos.

REMEMBER

Simplicity

Relevancy

Action

Black and white

PHOTO TIPS

Remember the old rule, keep it simple. If you're going to take the photos yourself, choose a basic camera. The simpler it is, the better. You can take adequate and, with practice, good photos with a point-and-shoot camera.

Instead of trying to get everyone into a shot, include just a few people with some action. If necessary, crop the picture to improve the image. Leave space below the photo for the caption.

It is best to use black-and-white glossy photos (unless you are having the photos printed in color). Although your print shop can shoot from a color print, the results will not be as good as those from a black-and-white photo. If the photo you have is in color, you can have a photo lab make a black-and-white glossy print. There will be some loss of clarity since the picture will be two generations from the original.

With a nonreproducing blue pencil, indicate the photo's position in your layout. Tell the print shop whether or not the photo is to be reduced or enlarged and by what percentage. You can use masking tape to put the instructions on the bottom of the photo.

Set up a filing system for your photos and negatives. Include the names of the people in the photos, the subject of the photo, and the photo credit line.

Consider the photo's relevance, visual appeal, and technical qualities when selecting which photo to use with an article.

When deciding on the photo's relevance to the article, ask yourself the following questions: Is there a reason to include the photo? Will it increase the reader's understanding and interest in the message you are trying to convey?

APPEALING FACTORS

Identity of subjects

Emotion of subjects

Composition

Action

VISUAL APPEAL

A number of factors determine visual appeal. The subject of the photo should be easy to identify. The reader who has to struggle to decipher what the picture is supposed to be will become frustrated. Photos of people expressing emotion have strong reader appeal. Emotion engages the reader's attention and strikes a responsive chord.

A well-balanced composition will be appealing. Composition means the arrangement of the subject of the photo and of other people or objects in the picture. Trust your instincts on what is pleasing to you, and you will usually be right.

Action adds to visual appeal. When including action shots, try to get those that show something about to happen. It is more appealing to see the pole vaulter arching over the bar than hitting the mat after completing the vault.

AVOID

Mug shots

Grip-n-grin

Committee shots

AVOID BORING SHOTS

There are no two ways about it: mug shots, grip-n-grin, and committee shots are boring. If you must include them, try to be creative.

Mug shots are head-and-shoulders portraits. They are usually stiff and formal. Instead of using them, try to include some action. Show the person performing a job. Encourage the person to use hand gestures, and try to elicit some facial expression. Avoid the talking into the phone ploy.

You have seen the grip-n-grin shot thousands of times, simply because the person taking the photo was told to take it that way or because the photographer couldn't think of anything more creative. Instead of the grip-n-grin, take a candid photo immediately after a presentation is made, or show the recipient being congratulated by family or friends.

The group or committee shot is another hackneyed pose. Try to pose group members informally. The closer they are to each other, the closer the photographer can get. One advantage is that the faces will appear larger in the photo. If you name the people in the caption, but their faces are unrecognizable, there is no point to having the photo. It will only frustrate your readers—and the people in the photo as well—and generate negative public relations.

TECHNICAL QUALITIES

The photo's technical qualities include correct contrast, focus and appropriate grain. Contrast between colors and shades of black, white, and gray affect clarity. It is best to have photos with a full range of grays, from light to dark, and clear blacks and whites. Avoid photos with only gray tones and no blacks or whites. Also avoid those with only black-and-white areas and no in-between tones of gray.

The image should be sharp, not blurred. The most important element of the photo should be in focus. The eyes are the most important feature in a photo of a person.

Grain means the small, curved particles of silver halide that make up the photo image. Grain is usually too fine to be visible without using a magnifying glass. If you have a photo enlarged, the grain will be more pronounced. The greater the enlargement, the larger the grain. Large grain creates a blotchy appearance in gray areas. Make sure the photos you use are without noticeable grain, unless you are using graininess to create a special effect. A glossy, rather than matte, finish will reproduce better.

Although the printer can use a photo that is larger or smaller than the final photo, it is preferable to reduce a larger print than to enlarge a smaller one. Reducing improves the sharpness of the image and softens edges. With enlargement, some definition of the image will be lost. Avoid enlarging a photo by more than 200%. You may prefer to work with 8-by-10-inch prints; they are large enough to show detail and hard to misplace. However, a 5-by-7 or 4-by-5-inch print will be adequate in most cases.

WORKING WITH THE PHOTO LAB

If a photo lab will be enlarging a photo for you, indicate the negative number or frame number that appears on the margin of the negative. Include the number of prints you want and the size of each.

Indicate the type of finish you want (usually glossy) and the weight of the photographic paper. Single- and double-weight are two common types. Single-weight is less expensive and probably will be adequate for your publication work.

Specify whether it is to be full frame or cropped. Full frame means that all of the image is printed; cropped means that some of the image has been eliminated. It is usually better to have the lab do full-frame enlargements. You can then crop the photo yourself and decide how you want the image to look. If the lab crops it, you limit your options.

CHARTS

Charts are another graphic form. There are four basic types: bar, pie, line, and table charts.

Use charts to highlight statistics that would otherwise be buried in the body of the article.

BAR CHART
The bar chart is used to represent quantities. A bar or column is used to represent each quantity. This type of chart can be used to highlight individual figures rather than the overall flow. It is useful to show the difference between two or more sets of figures charted over the same period of time. However, it is not effective if you have many numbers to compare. See Figure 9-1.

LINE CHART
The line chart uses a rising and falling line to represent changes in quantities plotted over a period of time. Use it to show a set of figures over the same time period—for example, the change of circulation figures over a week or more. The line chart is not effective when the information is too close together statistically or when there is little variation between quantities.

See Figure 9-2.

PIE CHART
The pie chart divides a whole into parts, usually expressed in percentages. You might use it to show the percentage of your collection devoted to different broad subject areas or age

FIGURE 9-1   Bar Chart

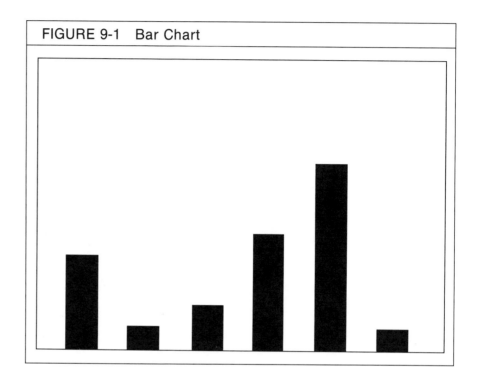

FIGURE 9-2   Line Chart

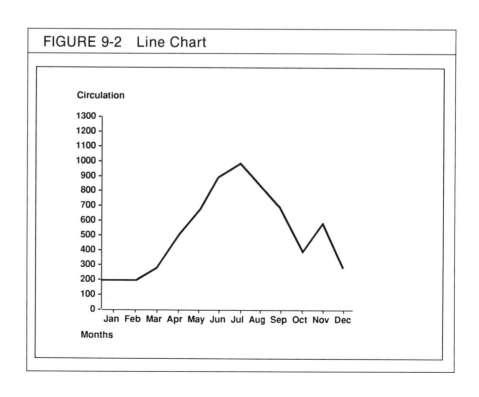

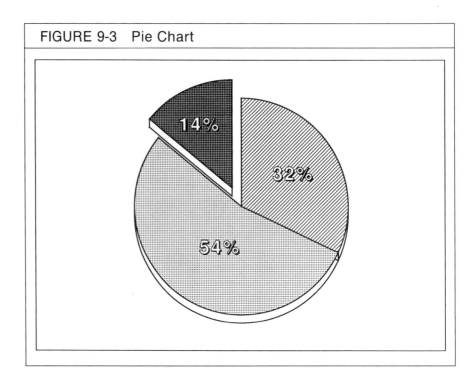

FIGURE 9-3   Pie Chart

FIGURE 9-4   Table Chart

School	No. of Students	No. of Books	No. of Periodicals	No. of Newspapers
Lincoln High	1,762	15,620	45	20
Jefferson High	243	2,430	21	10
Memorial Elem.	161	2,610	10	5
Community Elem.	493	3,930	20	2
Southwest Mid.	679	5,790	31	8
Total for District	3,338	28,380	127	45

groups, for example. It is not effective when dividing up the pie results in many small slices.

See Figure 9-3.

TABLE

Tables are used to display numbers or words arranged in columns. Use one when the numbers or words you want to compare are too numerous to be easily charted. A calendar is an example of a table. Tables are effective when the numbers or words must be read, not illustrated as an overall flow. If you can plot the statistics as a chart, don't use a table.

See Figure 9-4.

CONCLUSION

Graphics can add interest and pizzazz to your publication. They can also be time-consuming and expensive.

After you have designed, written, edited, and composed your newsletter, brochure, pamphlet, or flyer, you complete the process by creating a camera-ready copy.

If you are using desktop publishing, most of your layout will be done using the computer. The actual steps are dependent on which software package you are using. If you are not using desktop publishing, you will do your layout by hand.

Regardless of which method you choose, there are certain materials and tools you will use in pasting up your newsletter.

10 LAYOUT AND PASTE UP

"Cut and paste . . ."

Layout is arranging the text, white space, and graphics on paper. Paste up is attaching the text, headlines, and graphics to paper. Previous chapters have covered various elements of layout. This chapter tells you how to paste up the publication in order to create a camera-ready copy.

Local office supply and art stores are sources for most of the basic materials and tools you will need.

MATERIALS AND TOOLS

When you are getting ready to paste up your publication, have the following materials available.

- A supply of clean, smooth, white paper.
- A jar of rubber cement.
- A bottle of rubber cement thinner.
- A roll of masking tape.
- A bottle of correction fluid.
- A nonreproducing blue pencil.
- Fine-tipped felt marker pens.
- An art gum or plastic eraser.
- Sheets of tracing paper.
- Dry pressure-sensitive lettering if you intend to use larger letters for headlines.

The basic tools you will need are:

- An electric typewriter, preferably with a correcting feature and different type elements.
- A pair of scissors.
- A T-square ruler.

- A triangle.
- An X-acto knife.
- A stylus to use in transferring the rub-off lettering.

DESIGN GUIDELINES

Use white space to visually break up the text and graphics. White space increases the readability of the material and prevents eye fatigue. Use text, graphics, and white space to achieve balance. Make a copy of your tentative layout on a copy machine and look at it to see how the words, graphics, and white space work together. Change it until the composition appears balanced.

Leaving a half-inch margin around the page will help achieve a clean, balanced look.

Before pasting up your publication, decide on the kind of fold and the number of columns you will have, and whether it will be a one- or two-sided publication.

ROUGH PASTE UP

Type the text and, if necessary, crop any graphics you plan to use and indicate the percentage of reduction or enlargement for the print shop.

Position the articles, photos or graphics, and headlines, using a T-square to help you measure the distance from the edge of the paper to the item. Line them up, leaving equal left and right margins.

Draw faint guidelines with a light blue nonreproducing pencil around the corners of each item once it is aligned. Glue each item in place with rubber cement.

Next, touch up the edges, covering any smudges or marks with correction fluid.

Proofread your newsletter a final time, making additions, deletions, and substitutions by pasting new copy over existing material.

If you have additional instructions on photo cropping for the print shop, use the blue nonreproducing pencil to put them on the paste-up mechanical you are making.

Remember to paste the pages up in the correct order. (Chapter 8 covers this in detail.)

GRID SYSTEM

You can also do your layout and paste up using preprinted paper with grids. The grid lines, which are printed in a light blue, will not show up when reproduced. The preprinted grid makes it easier to align the copy, graphics, and headlines. Nine examples of grid patterns are shown in the following pages.

Example 10-1 shows a one-column format on an 8½-by-11-inch page. The column is 39 picas wide and 54 picas deep. The top, bottom, left, and right margins are 6 picas. This is a good format for a simple, typed newsletter. Because the line is so long, use a 10 pitch font to keep from having too many characters per line. (Remember, 10 pitch has 10 characters to an inch and 12 pitch has 12 characters to an inch.)

Example 10-2 illustrates a two-column format on an 8½-by-11-inch page. The right column is wider than the left and is where the text will be positioned. The left column is for quotes, graphics, and sidebars. The wider column is 28 picas wide; the narrower one is 10 picas. The columns are 54 picas deep, with 1-pica space between them. A 6-pica margin is used all around the page. This format is a good one for a typed newsletter and will work well with a 10 or 12 pitch font.

Example 10-3 has two columns of equal size on an 8½-by-11-inch page. The columns are each 20 picas wide and have a 2-pica divider. The left, right, and top margins are 4½ picas; the bottom margin is 6 picas. The column is 56½ picas deep. You can easily use this format for a typed or typeset newsletter.

Example 10-4 has three columns on an 8½-by-11-inch page. The left column is narrower than the other two: 9 picas wide. The other two are 16 picas each. The columns are 59 picas deep, and each column is divided by 1½ picas. The top margin is 4 picas; the left, right, and bottom margins are 3½ picas. The narrow column can be used for quotes, photos, or headlines, or can be left blank. It can always be on the left side, or the narrow column can always appear on the outer edge of the page. This format works well for typed or typeset newsletters. Use a 12 pitch font if you are using typewriter type.

Example 10-5 has three columns of 14 picas each with a 1½-pica space between columns. It is 58½ picas deep and has top, left, and right margins of 3 picas; the bottom margin is 4½ picas. This format works well for most typeset newsletters with 12 pitch type.

EXAMPLE 10-1   A Simple One-Column Grid

EXAMPLE 10-2   An Asymmetrical Two-Column Format

EXAMPLE 10-3   Two Equal Columns

EXAMPLE 10-4   An Asymmetrical Three-Column Format

69

EXAMPLE 10-5   Three Equal Columns

Example 10-6 divides an 8½-by-11-inch page into 12 boxes of 13½ picas by 13½ picas. There is a 1½-pica space between each box. The left and right margins are 3¾ picas; the top margin is 3 picas; and the bottom is 4½ picas. The column is 58½ picas deep. This is a good format if you anticipate using numerous graphics or photos.

Example 10-7 is an 8½-by-11-inch page divided into 36 boxes of 6½-by-9-picas with a 1-pica space between the boxes. The columns are 59 picas deep, and the margins are 3½ picas. The 36 boxes equal three columns with 14 picas each or six columns with 6½ picas each. This format is another one that works well with numerous photos. You might use this if you plan to include a number of individual pictures. If you size the photos to fit with the boxes, the proportions will turn out well.

Example 10-8 has four columns of 10½ picas each with a 1-pica space between the columns on an 8½-by-11-inch page. The column depth is 58½ picas. The left, right, and top margins are 3 picas; the bottom margin is 4 picas. This narrow-column format does not work well with a typewriter-produced newsletter. You would use this format with a typeset newsletter with a fairly small typeface such as an 8 or 9 point type.

Example 10-9 has three columns of 12½ picas each, with a fourth narrower column of 6 picas. The columns are 59 picas deep, with a 1-pica space between each column. The page is 8½-by-11-inches. The left and bottom margins are 2½ picas; the right margin is 2 picas; and the top margin is 4½ picas. This format is not recommended for a typewriter-produced newsletter. The columns are too narrow, even with 12 pitch type. You can use the narrower column for captions, graphics, headlines, or quotes.

Once you have created your final layout and paste up, you have a camera-ready copy. If you prefer not to put the pages in order and paste them, you can have the print shop do the pasteup to create a camera-ready copy.

EXAMPLE 10-6   Twelve-Box Grid, Useful For Graphics

EXAMPLE 10-7   Thirty-Six Box Grid Allows Flexible Layouts

EXAMPLE 10-8   Four Even Columns Work Best With Small Type

EXAMPLE 10-9   Asymmetrical Four-Column Layout

11 PUBLIC RELATIONS

"Image, image, image . . ."

Many people confuse public relations with publicity, advertising, and marketing. Public relations is a management function encompassing the planning and carrying out of good relationships between an organization and all its publics. For the library it can include as simple an activity as handing out balloons to children when they check out their books.

Publicity is the use of spoken, written, or other materials to direct public attention to a person, place, or thing. Adding the library's name and logo to the balloons one passes out would be a form of publicity. Newsletters, brochures, pamphlets, and flyers can all be forms of publicity.

Advertising is used to focus public attention in order to encourage people to buy or use something. It may be paid or unpaid.

Marketing is an advertising strategy used to promote an idea or sell a product. In recent years, attention has been focused on the necessity of "marketing" the library. Although many librarians have felt they lacked marketing skills, librarians have been involved in creating goodwill between their library and patrons for years.

CREATING AN IMAGE

The image you project for the library can be a powerful public relations tool. When you design a newsletter or promotional piece such as a flyer or brochure, keep in mind what image you want to convey for the library.

Do you want to create an awareness of professionalism? The feeling of a warm, welcoming, and friendly haven? The awareness of an energetic, up-to-date information base?

These quite different impressions can be developed by using the following techniques.

Establish a writing style consistent with the image you want to project and select graphics and typeface styles that

USER NEEDS

Physical comfort

Social interaction

Project completion

Research information

reinforce the chosen image. Choose words that convey the tone you want. Slant the information included in the publication towards the image you want projected.

To decide what image the library is to have, you need to understand what motivates the people who use the library and to clarify the library's goals.

What are your patrons' values and needs? What are their attitudes, lifestyles, and interests?

USING PROMOTIONAL PIECES

You might create promotional pieces that address such needs of your patrons as physical comfort, social interaction, project completion, research, and the need for helpful and informed staff.

One promotional piece could provide information on hours, location, availability of typing or computer rooms, use of study carrels or study rooms, availability of meeting or conference rooms, and locations of lounges, restrooms, and water fountains.

For those who are project oriented, location of copy machines, fax machines, coin changers, and tables where they can spread out their work would be helpful.

Researchers would be interested in knowing where reference materials are located, what rules apply to their use, and whom to see for further assistance.

Those looking for a social setting would be interested in the times and types of programs held, planned group activities, and the locations of conversational lounges.

It is important to strike a balance between the interests and needs of the users and those of the library.

USING A NEWSLETTER

A newsletter is one way to initiate your own controlled publicity. You can make it the library's voice. In order to develop an image, you must believe in and have pride in what you are doing. You need to be willing to adapt your image to changing times and situations, too. Look at the newsletter or publication through your readers' eyes. What does it say to them when they pick it up? Is it interesting, exciting, professional? Does it generate a feeling of friendliness and warmth? Is it informative, entertaining, and helpful? Decide what you want to communicate to the readers, then develop the image that will convey the message.

BROCHURES AND FLYERS

A brochure will last if printed on sturdy paper. Keep the size of the brochure in mind when designing it. One that will fit into a standard envelope is easier to work with than an odd-sized one. It can easily be mailed out to users in an envelope or as a self-mailer. It fits into standard information racks and is easier for the patron to slip in a bag or book than an odd-sized one.

Special-event flyers may be the size of a standard sheet of paper or smaller. Larger sizes can be useful, although generally they are more awkward to handle than the 8½-by-11-inch sheet of paper. They do not need to be printed on sturdy paper since they are used to publicize an event then discarded once the event is over. Use graphics and other visuals to draw attention to the flyer and the event. Limit the amount of information given. Include only the essentials.

Service flyers have a longer life, especially if they offer instruction on services that are always available. Emphasize factual information over image information in this kind of flyer. These are all ways of creating a positive image of your library.

12 BULK MAIL

"It's in the mail . . ."

Most of your publications will be handed out in the library or distributed through groups and meetings. If you need to use bulk mail, the pieces of mail must be second-, third-, or fourth-class mail.

Newsletters, brochures, and pamphlets generally will be bulk third-class mail. This kind of mail must weigh less than 16 ounces and may not contain a personal message.

The steps involved in bulk mailing are:

- Pay an annual bulk mail rate fee.
- Select the method of postage payment you will use.
- Make certain the pieces meet the preparation requirements of the Post Office.
- Sort the pieces by ZIP Code.
- Put them in bundles according to Post Office regulations.
- Attach labels in accordance with Post Office instruction.
- Put them in sacks and take them to your designated Bulk Mail Acceptance Unit.

The ways of paying the postage for third-class bulk mailings are: meter stamps, precanceled stamps, precanceled envelopes, and a permit imprint.

A postage meter is used to affix meter stamps to pieces of mail. You get a license from the Post Office for the use of a postage meter.

If you don't have a meter, you can use precanceled stamps. The permit for precanceled stamps can be obtained from the Postal Mailing Requirements Office.

The permit imprint method is the most commonly used since it is the most convenient. To use the permit imprint, it is necessary to establish a postage account at your Post Office.

Bulk-rate mailings can be presented only to the Post Office in the city where you obtained the permit. Of course, there are forms to fill out. First you have to get a special rate authorization for nonprofit organizations from the Postal Service. You will need a separate authorization from each Post Office where you plan to deposit special-rate mailings.

Next, you must apply for the method of payment you will use. Form 3601, "Application to Mail Without Affixing Postage Stamps," is used for approval to enter mail without using postage stamps. Form 3601-A, "Application for a Postage Meter License," is used to get a postage meter. Form 3620, "Permit to Use Precanceled Stamps or Government Precanceled Stamped Envelopes Application," is used to get pre-cancelled stamps or envelopes. (Examples of these forms are included in Appendix B.)

Each time you do a mailing, you have to fill out a Statement of Mailing. Form 3602, "Statement of Mailing with Permit Imprints," is used with permit imprint mailings. Form 3602-PC, "Statement of Mailing Bulk Rates," is used for precanceled stamp or metered postage mailings. (Examples of these forms are included in Appendix B.)

There are certain supplies you will need. Special pressure-sensitive labels are required, and are available from the Bulk Mail Acceptance Unit. The labels are coded "D," "C," "3," "S," and "MS." The label you use is determined by which type of bundle the pieces are put in. For example, the "D" label is used for bundles with ten or more pieces with the same ZIP Code.

You must use Post Office–approved rubber bands that measure $3\frac{3}{8}'' \times \frac{1}{4}''$. These are also available from the Bulk Mail Acceptance Unit.

You must use No. 3 gray canvas sacks, which are available at your local Post Office. You also need sack labels. Get blank sack labels from the Bulk Mail Acceptance Unit. Preprinted sack labels can be ordered from your account representative at the Bulk Mail Acceptance Unit.

A ZIP Code book may be useful. *The National ZIP Code Directory* is revised each year and can be purchased from any main Post Office as well as from classified stations and branches.

To qualify as a bulk mailing, there must be at least 200 pieces or 50 pounds of mail. The pieces must be presorted in ZIP Code order according to bulk mailing preparation requirements. You will receive instructions explaining the preparation requirements in detail.

Mailing lists can be produced and maintained by using database management software, by typing lists on special forms that can be photocopied onto pressure-sensitive labels, or by typing the labels with a typewriter.

Check with the administration to see if your organization already has a bulk mailing permit. If it does, find out which department handles the mail out and send your publication to them. Otherwise, if you need to do a large mailing, consider getting a bulk-rate mailing permit for the library.

CONCLUSION

Creating a newsletter, brochure, or pamphlet requires thought, planning, and attention to detail. With the guidelines in this manual and practice, you can create an interesting, attractive, and well-written publication.

BIBLIOGRAPHY

Baeckler, Virginia Van Wynen. *PR For Pennies: Low Cost Library Public Relations.* Hopewell, N.J.: Sources, 1978.

Carson, James. "Desktop Publishing: A Technology Waiting in the Wings." *Library Association Rec.*, Feb. 1988, 90, No. 2, 95–97.

Cole, Margaret and Sylvia Odenwald. *Desktop Presentations.* New York: American Management Assn., 1990.

Cook, Donald H. "The School Newsletter: Effective K-12 Communicator, A Practical Look at Preparing Newsletters for the Community." *School Library Media Quarterly*, Spring 1986, 14, 131–132.

Crawford, Walt. "Common Sense Wordworking: Writing with a Personal Computer." *Library Hi Tech*, Spring 1986, 4, No. 1, 73–84.

Cullinan, Bernice E. "Latching on to Literature: Reading Initiatives Take Hold." *School Library Journal*, Apr. 1989, 35, No. 8, 27–31.

Edsall, Marian S. *Practical PR For School Library Media Centers.* New York: Neal-Schuman Publishers, Inc., 1984.

Edwards, Karlene K. "Principals' Perceptions of Librarians: A Survey." *School Library Journal*, Jan. 1989, 35, No. 5, 28–31.

Gothberg, Helen M. "Understanding Marketing—Or Why You Can't Sell Libraries Like Kitty Litter." *Library Administration and Management*, Mar. 1987, 1, No. 2, 56–60.

Gray, Kenon. "Electronic P.R. for Media Centers." *Indiana Media Journal*, Summer 1986, 8, 3–5.

Hudson, Howard P. *Publishing Newsletters*, Rev. ed. New York: Scribner, 1988.

Hutchinson, Barbara. "School Library Scheduling: Problems and Solutions." *School Library Journal*, Dec. 1986, 33, No. 4, 30–33.

Kovitz, Nancy R. "An Abstracting Newsletter." *Library Journal,* 15 Feb. 1989, 114, No. 3, 138–139.

Latshaw, Patricia H. "The Janus Profession: Public Relations—Looking Out and Looking In." *Library Administration and Management,* Summer 1989, 3, No. 3, 118–121.

Leerburger, Benedict A. *Marketing the Library.* (Professional Librarian Series). Boston: G.K. Hall, 1982.

Liebold, Louise C. *Fireworks, Brass Bands, and Elephants: Promotional Events with Flair for Libraries and Other Nonprofit Organizations.* Phoenix: Oryx Press, 1986.

Peterson, Donna L. "What's All This I Hear About Information Power?" *Nebraska Library Association Quarterly,* Summer 1989, 20, 6–7.

Reck, Lawrence. "Developing a Public Relations Program." *Indiana Media Journal,* Winter 1989, 11, 29–32.

Rottmann, Clara Thoren. "The Marketing Process: Library Media Centers." *Nebraska Library Association Quarterly,* Summer 1989, 20, 7–10.

Russo-Martin, Elaine, and Suzanne F. Grefsheim. "How to Publish a Library Newsletter." *Medical Reference Services Quarterly,* Winter 1984, 3, No. 4, 27–34.

Sherman, Steve. *ABC's of Library Promotion,* 2nd ed. Metuchen, N.J.: Scarecrow, 1980.

Vaccaro, Bill. "Desktop Publishing and Public Libraries." *Public Libraries,* Summer 1988, 27, No. 2, 101–102.

Williams, James B., and Lawrence E. Murr. "Desktop Publishing: New Right Brain Documents." *Library Hi Tech,* Spring 1987, 5, No. 1, 7–13.

GLOSSARY

Accordion fold. A term used for two or more parallel folds that open like an accordion.

Alignment. How text lines up on a page or in a column.

Baseline. An invisible line on which type characters such as a and b rest; letters such as p and q extend below the baseline.

Blue nonreproducing pencil. A blue lead pencil used to indicate corrections or changes on galley proofs; the blue marks will not show when the sheet is reproduced.

Camera-ready copy. Text and graphics in final form, ready for the printer to photograph.

CAP. Acronym for computer-aided publishing.

Caption. A brief explanation that identifies an illustration or photograph.

C/lc. Caps and lowercase. Short for capital and lowercase characters.

Character. Term used for a letter, number, or punctuation mark.

Clip art. Camera-ready drawings on various subjects. See "copyright-free art."

Cold type. Typesetting that does not use molten lead or hot metal.

Collate. Assembling pages of a publication in sequence.

Column inch. The amount of text that will fit within the width of the column, one inch deep.

Content editing. Analyze and organize the information in the article; determine what information should be added or deleted to improve and enhance the text.

Copy. Text in manuscript, galley, or page proof form that will be arranged for printing reproduction.

Copy editing. Checking for faulty grammar, factual errors, and inconsistency in writing style.

Copy fitting. Calculating how many column inches typed copy will take up once it is typeset, or how much typed copy is needed to fill a fixed amount of column space.

Copyright-free art. Artwork that is not copyrighted and can be reproduced as needed.

Cropping. The act of emphasizing the main portion of the graphic or photograph by trimming material from its outer parts or placing black or red pencil marks at its margins and corners to show what portion to reproduce.

Desktop computers. Another name for a personal or microcomputer that can fit on a desktop.

Desktop publishing. Coined in 1985 by Paul Brainerd, a Seattle graphic artist and founder of Aldus Corporation, this phrase is used to describe the use of a personal computer, software program, and printer to produce publications without the use of typesetters, graphic artists, and paste-up specialists. It allows the user to have complete control over all of the page design elements of the publication.

Disk. A computer memory storage device.

Drilling. Punching holes in a publication for placement in a binder.

Editing. Art of generating, selecting, compiling, and revising literary, photographic, or audiovisual material to render it suitable for publication/production.

File. Collection of information stored as records.

Flat. A sheet of paper with negatives taped in position for making an offset printing plate.

Floppy disk. A disk made of nonrigid material on which computer data are stored.

Font. A complete set of characters in the same typeface; includes letters, punctuation, and symbols.

Format. Refers to all the physical qualities of a newsletter, brochure, or pamphlet, including shape, size, typeface, paper quality, and margin width.

Galley proof. Printed copy in the type size and column width of the newsletter's format; pages are not cut to size, but are long, narrow sheets used for proofreading.

Gate fold. Folding a sheet of paper with two parallel folds to form a center panel with non-overlapping foldouts on either side.

Graphic. Information presented in the form of pictures or images; computer graphics are created by using a computer to manipulate data in the form of pictures.

Grid. A design technique used to allocate space for text, photos, and white space by dividing the page into rectangular patterns.

Gutter. The margin on the binding, or inside, edge of a page.

Halftone. A broad class of illustrations (such as photographs, paintings, and pencil drawing with shading) that contain gradations of tones. They are more complex and expensive to reproduce than line illustrations.

Hard copy. Paper printout of computer data.

Hardware. The machines that make up a computer system.

Hot type. Typesetting by using molds for each character and pouring hot metal into lines of type.

Input. Data entered into a computer for processing.

ISSN. An acronym for International Standard Serial Number. The eight-digit ISSN identifies a periodical title.

Justify. Aligning lines of type on the right as well as on the left.

Kerning. The process of decreasing the amount of space between certain letter combinations in order to create visually consistent spacing among all the letters.

Laser printer. A letter-quality computer printer that uses laser technology.

Layout. Arranging text and graphics on a sheet to show the relative position of articles, illustrations, photos, and open space; serves as a guide for the printer.

Leading. Pronounced "ledding." The amount of white space between lines of type on a typeset page. The term comes from the technique of placing pieces of lead on a tray of metal type to create spaces.

Letter fold. A sheet folded with two parallel folds that make three overlapping panels, as in a typical business letter fold.

Letter-quality. Printed computer output that looks as if it were created with a typewriter.

Line illustration. A broad class of illustrations, composed entirely of solid black areas or lines on a white background. They are the simplest, least expensive type of illustration to reproduce.

Logo. Short for logotype. A trademark or identifying symbol of an organization or publication.

Mail merge. Merges names and addresses in one computer file with form letters in another file to produce a personalized letter.

Masthead. The box that lists the name and address of the organization, people responsible for the production of the newsletter, publication schedule, and copyright information.

Mechanical. A camera-ready paste up combining type and graphics, usually on a cardboard backing.

Memory. The part of a computer where data and instructions are stored.

Mouse. A small gizmo attached to the computer with a cable that can be rolled across the surface of a desk, thereby moving the cursor on the screen.

Nameplate. Name of the newsletter represented in type and/or illustration on the front page.

Offset camera. A method of printing which is chemical, indirect, and uses a flat plate surface specially treated to accept ink in image areas but not in non-image areas.

Output. The information a computer generates as a result of its calculations.

Paste up. A facsimile of the appearance of the printed newsletter, brochure, or pamphlet.

Personal computer. A computer small and inexpensive enough for a person to buy and keep at home.

Photocomposition. A method of typesetting by light exposure to film or paper.

Pica. A printing unit of measure. There are 12 characters to one inch in pica.

Point. A printing unit of measure, equal to $\frac{1}{12}$ of a pica or about $\frac{1}{72}$ of an inch.

Printer. Device that takes computer output and converts it into printed images.

Printing service. A commercial printing company that provides services such as typesetting, reproduction, binding, and bulk mailing preparation.

Proofreading. The process of reading composed copy in order to identify and correct errors.

Ragged. Leaving one or both sides of a column, or the bottom of columns across a page, uneven.

Readability. Refers to the facility with which an item can be read.

Resolution. The number of dots per inch that make up a character or graphic on a computer monitor screen. The higher the number of dots per inch (dpi), the sharper the image.

Rough. A rough sketch of a full-size page layout.

Rules. Vertical or horizontal lines on a page.

Sans serif. Type that does not have a line (serif) crossing the main strokes of a letter.

Serif. The line crossing the main strokes of a letter in some type styles.

Sidebar. Set-off text containing brief information related to the main article of a newsletter.

Software. A set of programs concerned with the operation of a data processing system.

Specs. Commonly used abbreviation for specifications; the instructions a customer provides that enable a typesetter or printer to reproduce the publication in a particular format.

Stet. Proofreader's term for "let it stand." It is used when a word, sentence, or paragraph is deleted or altered and later changed back to the original.

Text. The body of an article.

T-square. A ruler shaped like a T.

Typeface. A style of type characterized by its size, shape, slant, height, and width.

Typo. Common abbreviation for typographical error.

Upper case. Term used for capital letters.

Word processing. Entering, editing, formatting, and printing using a computer software program and a microcomputer or a word processing machine.

Word processor. A machine dedicated to the application of word processing.

WYSIWYG. "What-You-See-Is-What-You-Get" (pronounced "whissywig"). A term used to describe a software program that accurately represents the appearance of printed documents on the screen.

APPENDIX A

SOURCES OF MICROCOMPUTER-RELATED INFORMATION

BUYING MICROCOMPUTER HARDWARE
Computer Buying Guide: Rating the Best Computers, Peripherals, and Software. Editors of Consumer Guide. New York: Signet.

Published annually by the editors of Consumer Guide; compares and rates computers, peripherals, and software.

Computers for Everybody: Buyer's Guide. Jerry Willis and Merl Miller. Beaverton, Ore.: Dilithium Press.

A good one-volume hardware buying guide; reviews are three to ten pages and include hardware details, software information, accessories, and peripherals. Check *Computer Books in Print* for the latest edition.

PRINTER COMPANIES
Apple Computer, Inc.
20525 Mariani
Cupertino, CA 95014

LaserWriter printers for the Macintosh and MS-DOS.

Hewlett-Packard Corporation
4 Choke Cherry Rd.
Rockville, MD 20850

LaserJet Series and PaintJet for MS-DOS.

Tektronix
P.O. Box 500
Beaverton, OR 90777

Color Image Printer for Macintosh and MS-DOS.

SOFTWARE DIRECTORIES
Software Encyclopedia, 2 vols. New York: R.R. Bowker.
  Equivalent of *Books in Print* for software.

Software Reviews on File. New York: Facts on File.
  Provides excerpts from recently published software reviews.

Whole Earth Software Catalog. Stewart Brand, ed. Garden
City, NY: Quantum Press/Doubleday.
  Straightforward and informative commentary on programs, books, magazines, online services, suppliers, and some hardware.

SOFTWARE ONLY COMPANIES
(Send a postcard requesting a catalog.)

IBM Personally Developed Software
The Directory
P.O. Box 3266
Wallingford, CT 06494

American Peripherals (Commodore 64, PET, and VIC-20 catalogs)
122 Bangor St.
Lindenhurst, NY 11757

Strictly Software (Apple and IBM software)
P.O. Box 338
Granville, OH 43023

FREE NEWSLETTERS ON MICROCOMPUTERS
RAG: Random Access
Computer Faire, Inc.
181 Wells Ave.
Newton, MA 02159

Silicon Gulch Gazette
345 Swett Rd.
Woodside, CA 94062

DIRECTORIES OF COMPUTER BOOKS

Computer Book Review. Comber Press, Box 37127, Honolulu, HI 96837.

Published monthly; provides brief reviews of about 30 computer and microcomputer books per issue.

Computer Books and Serials in Print. New York: R.R. Bowker.

Arranged much like *Books in Print*.

The Readers Guide to Microcomputer Books. Michael Nicita and Ronald Petrusha. Brooklyn, NY: Golden-Lee.

Although recent, this has become a classic source for evaluations and reviews of about 1,000 microcomputer books.

PUBLICATIONS

Desktop Publishing: Buyer's Guide and Handbook.
Bedford Communications, Inc.
150 Fifth Avenue
New York, NY 10011

ITC Desktop Publisher
2 Hammarskjold Plaza
New York, NY 10017

MacUser
950 Tower Lane
Foster City, CA 94404

MacWorld
501 Second Street
San Francisco, CA 94107

PC World
501 Second Street
San Francisco, CA 94107

PC Magazine
One Park Avenue
New York, NY 10016

PC Computing
80 Blanchard Road
Burlington, MA 01803

Personal Computing
Ten Holland Drive
Hasbrouck Heights, NJ 07604

Personal Publishing
    Hitchcock Publishing Company
    191 S. Gary Avenue
    Carol Stream, IL 60188

Publish
    MultiMedia Communications, Inc.
    501 Second Street
    San Francisco, CA 94107

APPENDIX B:
BULK MAIL

SAMPLE FORMS

U. S. POSTAL SERVICE
APPLICATION TO MAIL AT SPECIAL BULK THIRD-CLASS RATES

PART 1 - FOR COMPLETION BY APPLICANT SECTION A - APPLICATION

NOTE: PLEASE READ ALL INFORMATION IN SECTION B ON THE BACK OF THIS APPLICATION BEFORE COMPLETING THE FORM BELOW.

Instructions

A. Be sure that all information entered below is legible so that our records will show the correct information about your organization

B. Show the complete name of the organization in item 1. The name shown must agree with the name that appears on all documents submitted to support this application.

C. A complete address representing a physical location for the organization must be shown in item 2. When mail is received through a post office box, show your street address first and then the box number.

D. The name of the applicant in item 5 must be the name of the individual submitting the application for the organization. The individual must be an officer of the organization. Printers and mailing agents may not sign for the organization.

E. No additional categories may be added in item 6. You must qualify as one of the types of organizations listed in order to be eligible for special rates.

F. Be sure to sign the application in item 12.

G. The date shown in item 14 must be the date that you submit the application to the post office. **NO APPLICATION FEE IS REQUIRED**

Please be sure all information is complete. PLEASE TYPE OR PRINT LEGIBLY

1. Complete Name of Organization

2. Address of Organization (Street, Apt./ Suite No.)

3. City, State, ZIP+4 Code

4. (Area Code)/ Telephone No.

 (   )

5. Name of Applicant (must represent organization that is applying.)

6. Type of Organization (Check only one. See 'E' above.)

☐ (01) Religious ☐ (03) Scientific ☐ (05) Agricultural ☐ (07) Veterans ☐ (09) Qualified Political Committee

☐ (02) Educational ☐ (04) Philanthropic ☐ (06) Labor ☐ (08) Fraternal

7. Check whether this organization is for profit or whether any of the net income inures to the benefit of any private stockholder or individual.

☐ YES ☐ NO

8. Check whether this organization is exempt from Federal income tax. (If 'YES', attach a copy of the exemption issued by the Internal Revenue Service which shows the section of the IRS code under which the organization is exempt. If an application for exempt status is pending with the IRS, you must check the 'NO' box.)

☐ YES ☐ NO

9. POST OFFICE where authorization is requested and bulk mailings will be made (City, State, and ZIP+4 Code of Main Post Office)
NOTE: An authorization may NOT be requested at a station or branch of a post office.

10. If your organization has previously mailed at the special bulk rates, list the post offices where mailings were most recently deposited at these rates:

11. Has your organization had special bulk third-class rate mailing privileges denied or revoked? If you answered "YES", please list the post office (City and State) where an application was denied or an authorization was revoked:

☐ YES

☐ NO

I certify that the statements made by me are true and complete. I understand that if this application for authorization is approved, it may only be used for our organization's mail at the post office specified above, and that we may not transfer or extend it to any other mailer. I further understand that if this application is approved, a postage refund for the difference between the regular and special bulk rates may be made for only those regular bulk third-class mailings entered at the post office identified above during the period this application is pending, provided the conditions set forth in section 642.4, Domestic Mail Manual, are met.

12. SIGNATURE OF APPLICANT

13. TITLE

14. DATE

Willful entry or submission of false, fictitious or fraudulent statements or representations in this application may result in a fine up to $10,000 or imprisonment up to 5 years or both (18 U.S.C.1001)

PART 2 - POSTMASTER AT ORIGINATING OFFICE
This part should be completed at the time the application is filed with your office

1. Signature of Postmaster (or designated representative)

2. Date application was filed with your office (Round Stamp)

PS Form 3624, April 1987   *(Page 1 of 3)*

SECTION B - GENERAL INFORMATION

ELIGIBILITY CRITERIA
The special bulk third-class rates may be granted only to:
  a. the eight categories of nonprofit organizations specified in section A, item 6, on the front, and
  b. qualified political committees including the National and State committees of political parties as well as certain named congressional committees.

These organizations are defined in sections 623.23 and 623.3 of the Domestic Mail Manual (DMM), which may be reviewed at the local post office.

A nonprofit organization must be both **ORGANIZED** and **OPERATED** for a qualifying primary purpose that is consistent with one of the types of organizations in 623.23 DMM. Organizations which **incidentally** engage in qualifying activities will not qualify for special rates.

Not all nonprofit organizations may mail at the special rates. Section 623.4, DMM, lists certain organizations, such as business leagues, chambers of commerce, civic improvement associations, social and hobby clubs, governmental bodies, and others, which, although nonprofit, do not qualify for the special bulk rates.

APPLICATION PROCEDURES
  1. Only organizations may apply. Individuals may not apply.
  2. Only the **ONE** category in item 6 which best describes the **PRIMARY PURPOSE** of the organization must be checked.
  3. The application must be **SIGNED** by someone in authority in the organization, such as the president or treasurer. It must not be signed by a printer or mailing agent.
  4. The completed Form 3624 must be submitted to the post office where bulk mailings will be deposited. If the application is approved, the authorization will apply only at that post office.

THE FOLLOWING DOCUMENTS MUST BE SUBMITTED WITH THE COMPLETED APPLICATION:

  a. Evidence that the organization is **NONPROFIT** and that none of its net income inures to the benefit of any private stockholder or individual. Acceptable evidence includes:
     • an IRS letter of exemption from payment of Federal income tax OR,
     • if an IRS exemption letter is not available, a financial statement from an <u>independent</u> auditor, such as a Certified Public Accountant, substantiating that the organization is nonprofit (a statement from a member of the organization is not sufficient.)

  b. Documents which describe the organization's **PRIMARY PURPOSE** such as:
     • formative papers which state the purpose for which the group is **ORGANIZED**, such as the Constitution or Articles of Incorporation, and
     • materials that show how the organization actually **OPERATED** during the past 6-12 months and how it will operate in the future, such as bulletins, financial statements, membership forms, publications it produced, minutes of meetings, a listing of its activities.

WHAT MAY BE MAILED
An organization authorized to mail at the special rates may mail only **ITS OWN MATTER** at those rates. It may not delegate or lend the use of its special rate permit to any other person or organization.

COOPERATIVE mailings may be made at the special bulk rates **ONLY** when **EACH** of the cooperating organizations is individually **AUTHORIZED** to mail at those rates at the office where mailings are deposited.

PS Form 3624, April 1987   (Page 2 of 3)

POSTMASTER AT ORIGINATING POST OFFICE

All Post Offices

1. When you furnish the mailer with Form 3624, explain the regulations pertaining to special bulk third-class rate eligibility contained in Chapter 6, DMM.

2. Be sure the mailer has completed all items in SECTION A, PART 1 and your office has completed SECTION A, PART 2.

Associate Post Offices

3. Place a check in column 1 of the check list in SECTION C for each item on the application that has been correctly completed. Sign and date the check list in the area provided for the originating post office. (Note: any deficiencies must be corrected before the application is forwarded for review.)

4. Forward the completed application, check list, and all supporting documents (See SECTION B, Application Procedures) to the Supervisor of Mail Classification at your area Management Sectional Center (MSC). If you report directly to a Field Division, these documents must be forwarded to the Division Manager of Mailing Requirements for review.

Field Division / MSC

5. If your office is the originating post office for the application, be sure you have followed all instructions in items 1 and 2 above.

6. Complete columns 2 and 3 of the check list in SECTION C. Place a check in column 2 for each item on the application that has been correctly completed. Place a check in column 3 next to each item that is deficient on the application. Follow the instructions in items 3 or 4, below, as appropriate

FIELD DIVISION / MSC
REVIEW OF APPLICATIONS RECEIVED FROM ASSOCIATE OFFICES

1. Upon receipt of Form 3624 from an associate post office, check to be sure that the application and Column 1 of the post office check list are complete and proper supporting documents have been submitted.

2. Complete Columns 2 and 3 of the check list in SECTION C. Place a check in Column 2 for each item on the application that has been correctly completed. Place a check in Column 3 next to each item that is deficient on the application.

3. If the check list indicates the application in SECTION A is properly completed and proper attachments accompany it, forward the application, check list and attachments to the Rates and Classification Center (RCC) serving your area.

Disposition of Incorrect or Incomplete Applications by Division or MSC

4. If you are the originating post office and any items are checked in Column 3 of the check list, the deficiencies must be corrected before the application can be forwarded to the RCC.

5. If an application received from an associate post office is incomplete or deficient in any area, return it to the originating postmaster for correction of the deficiencies.

RCC'S
NOTIFICATION OF APPROVAL OR DENIAL OF APPLICATION

The Rates and Classification Center (RCC) serving the originating post office will notify the organization directly, by letter, whether its application has been approved or denied. The RCC will send the originating post office a copy of this ruling letter. The entire file, including the original application, will be returned to the originating post office with the copy of the ruling. The post office MUST retain the original application, letter of approval or denial, and all supporting documents in its files. (See DMM 642 for file retention period.) The RCC will also send a copy of the letter of approval or denial to the MSC or Field Division, as information. *(Page 3 of 3)*

SECTION C - POST OFFICE CHECK LIST FOR FORM 3624

NOTE: Part 1 and Part 2 of the Check List below refer to the items in SECTION A, Application. The ITEM #'s in the left column below correspond to the ITEM #'s on the Application.

Part 1 ITEM #		Orig. P.O. Col 1	MSC Div. Col 2	Deficient Col 3
1 - 5	All items are legible.			
1	Complete name of the organization is shown and matches the name shown in supporting documents.			
2 - 4	Complete address and phone number are shown			
5	A complete name is shown			
6 - 8	One choice has been checked in each line			
9	The ZIP+4 Code is shown for the post office			
12-14	The applicant signed and dated the application			

Part 2: ITEM #				
1 & 2	The postmaster signed and dated the application			

NOTE: The person at the originating post office that reviews the application should identify the following items in the file (e.g. IRS letter of exemption submitted as proof of nonprofit status) so that the RCC can easily locate them. You may use paper clips, rubber bands, slips of paper, etc. to identify these documents.

Organization submitted proof of nonprofit status			
Organization submitted statement of purpose (i.e. Articles of Incorporation., Constitution)			
Organization submitted proof of how it operates (e.g. newletters, minutes of meetings, etc.)			

The examiner at the originating post office and the examiner at the MSC or Division must sign and date this check list in the appropriate areas provided below before the application is forwarded to the RCC.

ORIGINATING POST OFFICE
City, State & Postmaster's ZIP+4 Code

Examiner's Signature

Telephone No. ( )	Date
☐ PEN ☐ COMM	

REVIEWING POST OFFICE - (MSC or FIELD DIVISION)
City, State & Postmaster's ZIP+4 Code:

Examiner's Signature

Telephone No. ( )	Date
☐ PEN ☐ COMM	

Application returned to Originating post office for correction/completion ☐	Application forwarded to RCC ☐

☆ U.S. Government Printing Office: 1987—183-713/69093

PS FORM 3601

U.S. POSTAL SERVICE
APPLICATION TO MAIL WITHOUT AFFIXING POSTAGE STAMPS

APPLICANT: File at office where mailings will be made with required fee.

NAME OF APPLICANT (Print or type) ①	APPLICANT'S TELEPHONE NO ②

ADDRESS OF APPLICANT (Street, Apt /Suite No., City, State and ZIP Code) (Print or Type) ③

AVERAGE NUMBER OF PIECES IN EACH MAILING ④	CLASS OF MAIL MATTER ☐ FIRST ⑤ ☐ SECOND ☐ THIRD ☐ FOURTH	SIGNATURE OF APPLICANT ⑥	DATE ⑦

TO BE COMPLETED BY POSTMASTER ▶	AMOUNT OF FEE COLLECTED $ ⑧	PERMIT NUMBER	DATE OF ISSUANCE

POSTMASTER: Retain application in your file. When approved, deliver authorization to permit holder.

PS Form 3601, July 1980

- -

U.S. POSTAL SERVICE
AUTHORIZATION TO MAIL WITHOUT AFFIXING POSTAGE STAMPS

You are authorized to mail at this post office matter bearing permit imprints, postage to be paid in money.

POST OFFICE (City, State and ZIP Code) ⑨

PERMIT NUMBER	DATE OF ISSUANCE	SIGNATURE OF POSTMASTER

NAME OF PERMIT HOLDER (Address, Apt /Suite No., City, State and ZIP Code)

TO:

SAMPLE

PS Form 3601

✿ U.S. G.P.O. 1982-654-243

PS FORM 3601-A

U.S. Postal Service		
APPLICATION FOR A POSTAGE METER LICENSE		
APPLICANT: File at office where mailings will be made. (Part 144, Domestic Mail Manual)		

Name of Applicant *(Print or type)* **(1)**	Applicant Telephone No. **(2)**
Address of Applicant *(Street, City, State, ZIP Code) (Print or type)* **(3)**	Federal Agency **(4)** Code Sub Code
Meter to be set at *(Main office, station, or branch)* **(5)**	Setting Location *ZIP Code* **(6)**
Signature of Applicant **(7)**	Date **(8)**
TO BE COMPLETED BY POSTMASTER *(Retain application in your file. After application has been approved, deliver authorization to license holder.)*	License Number	Date of Issuance

U.S. Postal Service		
LICENSE TO USE POSTAGE METERS		

You are authorized to pay postage on any class of mail by printing meter stamps with postage meters, subject to all conditions applying to the various classes of mail.

Post Office **(9)**	Date	License No.
Name of License Holder *(Address, City, State and ZIP Code)*		
		_____ *(Signature of Postmaster)*

SAMPLE

PS Form 3601-A, Dec. 1985 *(Detached)*

PS FORM 3620

U.S. POSTAL SERVICE

PERMIT TO USE PRECANCELED STAMPS OR GOVERNMENT PRECANCELED STAMPED ENVELOPES APPLICATION

APPLICANT: File with postmaster of office where mailings will be made. No fee is required to accompany this application, but mailers who present third-class matter in bulk under 622, Domestic Mail Manual, must pay the bulk mailing fee for each calendar year or part thereof.

1. NAME OF APPLICANT *(Print or type)*	TELEPHONE NO.	COMPLETE APPLICABLE PORTION(S)
		3. APPLICATION IS MADE FOR A PERMIT TO USE —
2. ADDRESS OF APPLICANT *(Print or type)* — NO. AND STREET / CITY, STATE AND ZIP CODE		☐ GOVERNMENT PRECANCELED STAMPED ENVELOPES *(Mailings must be of not less than 200 pieces at one time of third-class matter in bulk under 622, Domestic Mail Manual.)*
SIGNATURE OF APPLICANT		☐ PRECANCELED STAMPS *(Complete item 4 below)*
TO BE COMPLETED BY POSTMASTER ▶	PERMIT NUMBER	DATE OF ISSUANCE	4. CLASS OF MATTER ☐ FIRST ☐ SECOND ☐ THIRD ☐ FOURTH
POSTMASTER: Retain application in your file. After application has been approved, deliver authorization to permit holder.		DATE

PS Form **3620**
Dec. 1979

- -

PERMIT TO USE PRECANCELED STAMPS OR ENVELOPES

You are authorized to use precanceled stamps or envelopes on matter mailed at this post office under the conditions in 143. Domestic Mail Manual.

PERMIT NUMBER	DATE OF ISSUANCE
POST OFFICE, STATE AND ZIP CODE	SIGNATURE OF POSTMASTER

(Fill in name of permit holder and address below)

TO:

SAMPLE

PS Form **3620**

☆ U.S. Government Printing Office: 1985—461-869/22555

U.S. Postal Service **STATEMENT OF MAILING WITH PERMIT IMPRINTS**	MAILER: Complete all items by typewriter, pen or indelible pencil. Prepare in duplicate if receipt is desired. Check for instructions from your postmaster regarding box labeled "RCA Offices."	Permit No. **1**

Post Office of Mailing **2**	Date **3**	Receipt No.	Mailing Statement Sequence No.

Check applicable box   **4**

3rd Class
- ☐ Carrier Route
- ☐ Basic ZIP + 4
- ☐ 5-Digit ZIP + 4
- ☐ ZIP + 4 Barcoded
- ☐ 5-Digit
- ☐ Basic
- ☐ Single Piece

4th Class
- ☐ Library Rate
- ☐ Special 4th Class Single Piece
- ☐ Presort Special 4th Class

Processing Category *(See DMM 128)*   **5**
- ☐ Letters
- ☐ Flats
- ☐ Machinable Parcels
- ☐ Irregular Parcels
- ☐ Outside Parcels

Weight of a single piece   ___ . ___ ___ ___ lbs.   **6**

RCA Offices: **9**

TOTAL IN MAILING		NUMBER OF			
Pieces **7**	Pounds **8**	Sacks	Trays	Pallets	Other Containers

Name and Address of Permit Holder *(Include ZIP Code)*   **10**   **12**

Telephone No. **11**

☐ Check if nonprofit under DMM 623*

Name and Address of Individual or Organization for which mailing is prepared *(If other than permit holder)*   **13**

☐ Check if nonprofit under DMM 623*

Name and Address of Mailing Agent *(If other than permit holder)*   **14**

POSTAGE COMPUTATION   **15**

		No. Pounds	Rate/Pound $	Postage
Pound Rate	1. Pound Rate Postage Charge			

		No. Qual. Pieces	Rate Per Piece $	Postage
Piece Rates	2. ZIP + 4 Barcoded			
	3. 5-digit ZIP + 4			
	4. Basic ZIP + 4			
	5. Carrier Route			
	6. 5-digit			
	7. Basic			
	8. Rate Category	No. of Pieces	Rate Per Piece $	Postage
	9. SUBTOTAL (1 through 8) ▶			Postage

10. Additional Postage Payment *(State reasons for additional postage payment on reverse side under "Comments")*   ☐ See reverse side   **16** | No. of Pieces | Rate/Piece $ | Postage |

11. ☐ Check if applicable third-class bulk piece rate is affixed to each piece. *(Form 3602-PC required)*

12.   **17**   **TOTAL POSTAGE** *(9 plus 10)* where applicable ──────▶   Total Postage $

* The signature of a nonprofit mailer certifies that: (1) The mailing does not violate section 623.5 DMM; and (2) Only the mailer's matter is being mailed; and (3) This is not a cooperative mailing with other persons or organizations that are not entitled to special bulk mailing privileges; and (4) This mailing has not been undertaken by the mailer on behalf of or produced for another person or organization that is not entitled to special bulk mailing privileges.

The submission of a false, fictitious or fraudulent statement may result in imprisonment of up to 5 years and a fine of up to $10,000. (18 U.S.C. 1001) In addition, a civil penalty of up to $5,000 and an additional assessment of twice the amount falsely claimed may be imposed. (31 U.S.C. 3802)

I hereby certify that all information furnished on this form is accurate and truthful, and that this material presented qualifies for the rates of postage claimed.

Signature of Permit Holder or Agent *(Both principal and agent are liable for any postage deficiency incurred)*   **18**   Telephone No.

(THIS SECTION FOR POSTAL USE ONLY)

PS Form 3602-PC, Apr. 1988   FOR ZONE RATED MAIL USE FORM 3605   Side B

U.S. Postal Service **STATEMENT OF MAILING BULK RATES**	MAILER: Complete all items by typewriter, pen or indelible pencil. Prepare in duplicate if receipt is desired. Check for instructions from your postmaster regarding box labeled "RCA Offices."	Permit No. or Meter License No. **(1)**

Post Office of Mailing **(2)**	Date **(3)**	Receipt No.	Mailing Statement Sequence No.

Check applicable box (4)

3rd Class	4th Class
☐ *Carrier Route*	☐ *Library Rate*
☐ *Basic ZIP + 4*	☐ *Special 4th Class Single Piece*
☐ *5-Digit ZIP + 4*	☐ *Presort Special 4th Class*
☐ *ZIP + 4 Barcoded*	
☐ *5-Digit*	
☐ *Basic*	
☐ *Single Piece*	

Postage is being paid by: *(Check one)*   ☐ Precanceled Stamps   ☐ Meter Stamps **(5)**

Processing Category *(See DMM 128)* **(6)**

☐ *Letters*	☐ *Irregular Parcels*
☐ *Flats*	☐ *Outside Parcels*
☐ *Machinable Parcels*	

Weight of a single piece _ _ . _ _ _ _ lbs. **(7)**   RCA Offices:

TOTAL IN MAILING   **NUMBER OF (10)**

Pieces **(8)**	Pounds **(9)**	Sacks	Trays	Pallets	Other Containers

Name and Address of Permit Holder *(Include ZIP Code)* **(11)**	Telephone No. **(12)**	POSTAGE COMPUTATION

		No. Pounds	Rate/Pound $	Postage
Pound Rate	1. Pound Rate Postage Charge	No. Pounds	Rate/Pound $	Postage

☐ Check if nonprofit under DMM 623* **(13)**

Piece Rates **(16)**	2. ZIP + 4 Barcoded	No. Qual. Pieces	Rate Per Piece $	Postage
	3. 5-digit ZIP + 4	No. Qual. Pieces	Rate Per Piece $	Postage
	4. Basic ZIP + 4	No. Qual. Pieces	Rate Per Piece $	Postage
	5. Carrier Route	No. Qual. Pieces	Rate Per Piece $	Postage
	6. 5-digit	No. Qual. Pieces	Rate Per Piece $	Postage
	7. Basic	No. Qual. Pieces	Rate Per Piece $	Postage
	8. Rate Category	No. of Pieces	Rate Per Piece $	Postage
	9. SUBTOTAL (1 through 8) ▶			Postage

Name and Address of Individual or Organization for which mailing is prepared *(If other than permit holder)* **(14)**

☐ Check if nonprofit under DMM 623*

Name and Address of Mailing Agent *(If other than permit holder)* **(15)**

10. Additional Postage Payment *(State reasons for additional postage payment on reverse side under "Comments")* ☐ See reverse side **(17)**	No. of Pieces	Rate/Piece $	Postage

11. ☐ Check if applicable third-class bulk pound rate is paid by permit imprint. *(Form 3602 required)*

12. **(18)** TOTAL POSTAGE *(9 plus 10)* where applicable ⟶	Total Postage $

* The signature of a nonprofit mailer certifies that: (1) The mailing does not violate section 623.5 DMM; and (2) Only the mailer's matter is being mailed; and (3) This is not a cooperative mailing with other persons or organizations that are not entitled to special bulk mailing privileges; and (4) This mailing has not been undertaken by the mailer on behalf of or produced for another person or organization that is not entitled to special bulk mailing privileges.

The submission of a false, fictitious or fraudulent statement may result in imprisonment of up to 5 years and a fine of up to $10,000. (18 USC 1001) In addition, a civil penalty of up to $5,000 and an additional assessment of twice the amount falsely claimed may be imposed. (31 U.S.C. 3802)

I hereby certify that all information furnished on this form is accurate and truthful, and that this material presented qualifies for the rates of postage claimed.

Signature of Permit Holder or Agent *(Both principal and agent are liable for any postage deficiency incurred)* **(19)**	Telephone No.

(THIS SECTION FOR POSTAL USE ONLY)

PS Form **3602-PC**, Apr. 1988   FINANCIAL DOCUMENT — FORWARD TO FINANCE OFFICE

APPENDIX C

EXAMPLE OF PROOFREADER SYMBOLS

∧	Make correction indicated in margin
stet	Retain crossed-out word or letter, let it stand (stet)
¶	Make a paragraph here
trs or ∿	Transpose words or letters
ℓ	Delete words or letters indicated (dele)
ℓ	Take out the character indicated and close up
ℓ	Line drawn through a cap means lower case
⌒	Close up; no space
#	Insert a space here
Caps	Put in capitals
ital	Change to Italic
≡	Under letter or word means capital
—	Under letter or word means Italics
〰	Under letter or word means boldface
,/	Insert comma
ˇ ˇ	Insert quotation marks

There are a number of ways to indicate corrections. Common proofreading symbols, or marks, are one way. Most people are familiar with these and you should have little difficulty in making your corrections easily known.

APPENDIX D:
EXAMPLES OF LIBRARY NEWSLETTERS

LIBRARY LETTER

VOLUME IV   NUMBER 1

Effective 1-9-89!!!

The Library Processing Center will use a new address. Please use the following on all Purchase Orders with the LPC as the destination:

> Fort Worth ISD
> Library Processing Center
> 601 East Northside Dr.
> Fort Worth, TX 76106
>
> Telephone: 625-5709

FACT, FANTASY AND FUN

"Fact, Fantasy, and Fun in Children's Literature" is the theme of the annual Sam Houston State University Book Festival. The conference convenes at 5:30 on March 31 and continues through Saturday at 4:00 p.m. The program will feature author-illustrator, Gail Gibbons, Folklorist, Alvin Schwartz, Riddle King, Mike Thaler and Professional storyteller, Rafe Martin. Workshops which can be taken for AAT or CEU credit cover a wide range of topics of interest to elementary teachers and librarians. For more information, write the Department of Library Science, Sam Houston State University, Box 2236, Huntsville, Texas 77341. Registration: $35.00. Deadline: February 15.

SILVERWARE SURPLUS

Some visitors to the Heath abode during the holidays left various pieces of silverware. One very nice knife, with beaded pattern handle by Reed and Barton Stainless may have come with one of the cheese balls for the Librarian Social on December 6. A fork, also stainless is a rose pattern by Imperial. Both of these are in the possession of Martha in the Library Media Services office and may be claimed from there.

Children's Press Discount

Children's Press has agreed to give libraries ordering direct a 35% discount off list prices. If you wish to take advantage of that discount, you may order direct from Children's Press including the discount in the instructions to the vendor portion of the purchase order.

Weeding Maps

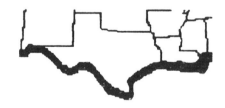

Recently, a question concerning weeding old maps was posed by a librarian. Library Media Services requested some guidelines for discarding maps from the Social Studies Program Director, Sy Karlin. The following guidelines were provided:

> Maps prior to 1970: If without historical significance, discard
>
> Maps after 1970: Use form #927 to transfer to #928

Reproducible:

Each month I ask teachers to share information with me about instructional units and projects. The form reproduced below facilitates this communication. There is space for teachers to request materials as well as services (instruction in library skills or audiovisual production, book lists, and so forth). I have used the form at both elementary and middle school levels. It's an easy way to let teachers know you're there to help—and also to let you keep track of requests!

—*Kathy Hedden, William Annin Middle School, Basking Ridge, New Jersey.*

Teacher _____ Date _____

WORKING · TOGETHER · CLASSROOM · LIBRARY-MEDIA CENTER

Please take a few minutes to complete this information request.

What major topics are your students studying this month?

_____
_____
_____
_____
_____

List any supplemental materials or services that may be needed. For example:

   Materials—books, tapes, filmstrips, computer software, videocassette tapes, etc.

   Services—research periods, booklists, library skills lessons, audiovisual production, computer use and instruction, materials gathered for classroom use.

_____
_____
_____
_____
_____
_____
_____

Your suggestions for additions to our library media center are always welcome. Any ideas?

_____
_____
_____
_____

Thank You!

Teacher _____ Date _____

WORKING · TOGETHER · CLASSROOM · LIBRARY-MEDIA CENTER

Please take a few minutes to complete this information request.

What major topics are your students studying this month?

_____
_____
_____
_____
_____

List any supplemental materials or services that may be needed. For example:

   Materials—books, tapes, filmstrips, computer software, videocassette tapes, etc.

   Services—research periods, booklists, library skills lessons, audiovisual production, computer use and instruction, materials gathered for classroom use.

_____
_____
_____
_____
_____
_____
_____

Your suggestions for additions to our library media center are always welcome. Any ideas?

_____
_____
_____
_____

Thank You!

FOOTNOTES

701 Angus Avenue West
San Bruno, California
(415) 877-8878

HOURS:

Monday - Thursday 10-9
Friday   10-6
Saturday   10-5
Closed Sundays and
Holidays

MARCH   1991

HOLIDAY HOURS: The Library will close at noon on Friday, March 29, in observance of Good Friday. We will be open our regular hours (10 - 5) on Saturday, March 30.

CHILDREN'S STORYTIME

Storytimes will begin again on March 18. The schedule is as follows:

Pajama Storytime: Monday nights, 7 - 7:30 p.m.
                       (March 18 - April 22)

Preschool Storytime: Tuesday mornings, 11 - 11:30 a.m.
                       (March 19 - April 23)

MARCH AFTER-SCHOOL SPECIAL

HERE'S CHUCK!! Come join us after class for a program of stories, songs and puppets with Chuck Ashton, **Thursday, March 14, at 4 p.m.**

REFERENCE HEADLINER

<u>LESKO'S INFO-POWER</u> **by Matthew Lesko (call no. R 353 L).** If information is power, what are the best sources of information? "The government is the largest source of information in the world," says Matthew Lesko, and only a tiny fraction of this wealth finds its way into your local library. <u>Lesko's Info-Power</u> lists more than 30,000 free and low cost government publications, programs, services, and experts that you can tap for information on almost any topic you can think of from banks and credit to climate forecasts to AIDS. Lesko also tells you how to locate government experts by phone, how to double check the information you get, and even gives telephone numbers to call if the phone numbers listed have been changed. This is a well organized, fun-to-read introduction to the world of government information sources.

WOMEN'S HISTORY MONTH DISPLAY

March is Women's History Month. This year our library foyer features a display on "Women and the Constitution". Today we think of the struggle for constitutional rights mainly in terms of the Equal Rights Amendment, but the discussion of women's legal rights goes back to the beginning of our country's history, when the issues were women's rights to own property, to divorce, to have free access to their children, and to vote.

The leaders of the women's suffrage movement were women originally active in the abolitionist cause, who found that they were second-class citizens even within the anti-slavery movement. They were active in promoting the 15th Amendment, which gave African American men the right to vote, but it was not until 1920, with the passage of the 19th Amendment, that women themselves were finally enfranchised. <u>Voices of the New Feminism</u> (call no. 301.412 V) provides a very readable overview of the evolution of women's rights in the United States. For more books on this topic, check the subject catalog under the following headings:

> WOMEN--LEGAL STATUS, LAWS, ETC.
> WOMEN--SUFFRAGE
> WOMEN--UNITED STATES--HISTORY
> WOMEN'S RIGHTS.

TEA TIME FOR TEACHERS

Volume II, Number 1   A publication of EARLY CHILDHOOD EDUCATION   October 1990

CONTENTS

TEA TIME FOR TEACHERS

FORT WORTH

INDEPENDENT SCHOOL DISTRICT

Pat Wright and Kay Moberg
Coordinators for
Early Childhood Education

Julie Miers
PAT Parent Educator

Carolyn Spitzer
Secretary

Ann Kinlough
PAT Clerk

Roberta Holiday
Newsletter Editor

POSITIVE REINFORCEMENT: GOOD OR BAD?

Praising the child to reinforce desired behaviors is accepted educational practice. Rewards and recognition are other examples of positive reinforcement. We would agree that praise and rewards are better than punishment for misbehavior and lack of motivation. However, there is another point of view.

An article in the DALLAS MORNING NEWS by Alfie Kohn (June 23, 1990, "The Risk of Rewards") cites research findings showing that positive reinforcement is not effective in motivating learning or in teaching children responsible conduct. According to A.S. Neill, a British educator, rewards suggest to the child that an activity is not worth doing for its own sake. The reward may actually inhibit doing a task out of intrinsic motivation. The reward itself becomes the goal.

Brandeis University professor Teresa Amabile says the child comes to think of the activity as something that is a means to the real end, the prize. The result is a narrow and superficial focus on a task, an approach that stifles high quality work. John Condry of Cornell University calls rewards "the enemies of exploration."

Why should there be such opposite views about positive reinforcement? Perhaps the explanation lies in our tendency to generalize and universalize effective strategies into "magic formulas." Praising or rewarding a child for positive reinforcement does not mean this is always the best strategy or that any type of praise or any reward is appropriate. It does not mean that the same things work with every age level and every child.

Clare Cherry, in PLEASE DON'T SIT ON THE KIDS (David S. Lake, 1983), points out that intrinsic motivation requires developmental growth. Adults need to guide and control children while providing increasing opportunities for children to exercise self-determination.

Chit Chat with Kay and Pat

Thank you for helping keep PREKINDERGARTEN and KINDERGARTEN, and the concept it names, as a setting in which young children are nourished and helped to grow through group activities, materials, and play. We are proud of the district's stance and commitment concerning early education. We stand tall in the state and nation on issues which impact our youngest citizens.

We look forward to working with you this year. We'll see you around ... in your building, at workshops, at professional meetings. You can reach us at 921-2823. We're here for you.

*****

Please come see us in the new early childhood education office. We are in Room 24A at the Alice Carlson Annex. We will have OPEN HOUSE for you on Tuesday, October 23, from 3:30 to 5:00 p.m. Join us for "tea".

*****

McGruff kits are available for kindergarten use in every school library.

*****

TEA TIME TATTLER

Virginia Brown, kindergarten teacher at Natha Howell, completed a master's degree in early childhood education in May, with ESL endorsement, at Texas Woman's University.

Dorothy MacMurray and Karla Stringfellow, preK teachers at Manuel Jara, were involved in an automobile accident three weeks ago. Dorothy is still out. Send her a card.

Dr. Debbie Coonrod, kindergarten teacher at Springdale, was named co-recipient of the Ethel M. Leach Award for service to education regionally and nationally. She was given a plaque and stipend, and her name was placed on a master plaque in the dean's office at TWU.

Some of the new names on faculty lists are not new teachers. Recently married are Rosie Estrada at Westcreek, now Mrs. Michael Luneau; Lisa Barlow at Hubbard, who became Mrs. Tim Nicholas; and Loma Ratcliffe at South Hi Mount, now Mrs. Fergueson (she honeymooned in Acapulco).

Marge Hughes, preK/kindergarten Montessori teacher at Glen Park, became Mrs. Robert Ackroyd. She and her husband toured the West Coast in July, and she missed the August birth of a granddaughter in Fontana, California.

Vicki Melton, formerly at Maude I Logan, became the mother of Carey Lynn, her second child, on June 13. Susan Staub at Glen Park is expecting twins, according to reporter Linda Shepard.

"Maybe I can bluff my way through."

newsline

Volume 7, Issue 4: April 1991
A Quarterly Publication of the Campbell County Public Library
2101 4-J Road, Gillette, Wyoming 82716   307-682-3223

NATIONAL LIBRARY WEEK
April 14 - 20

Reading is essential to leading a successful and productive life.

It is the single most effective skill people can use to learn, gather information, keep up with new developments in this rapidly changing world and communicate on a daily basis.

This year's National Library Week theme "Read. Succeed." puts the focus on libraries and literacy. Libraries across the country will be celebrating April 14-20.

The Campbell County Public Library will be celebrating National Library Week in many ways.   Be sure to check the Calendar of Events for all the details.

MARY HIGGINS CLARK

Thanks to a generous grant from the Mobil Foundation, represented locally by Mobil Coal Producing, Inc. Caballo Rojo Mine, the library is able to bring the distinguished mystery writer Mary Higgins Clark to Gillette for National Library Week.

Clark will be conducting a Creative Writing Mini Workshop on Friday, April 19, from 9:30 to 10:30 a.m. in the Wyoming Room. Seating is limited for this free workshop. Please call 687-0009 to register if you would like to attend.

Clark will speak to the public about her career Friday evening, April 19, beginning at 7:00 p.m. in the Wyoming Room. Admission is by free ticket only. Tickets will be available from the Circulation Desk of the library on Sunday, April 7.

Clark is one of America's top-selling authors, with more than 15 million copies of her books in print in the U.S. alone. She is the author of the bestsellers Where Are the Children?, A Stranger is Watching, The Cradle Will Fall, A Cry in the Night, Stillwatch, Weep No More, My Lady, While My Pretty One Sleeps, and The Anastasia Syndrome and Other Stories. Her new novel, Loves Music, Loves to Dance is due to be released the end of April.

The library would like to thank the Mobil Foundation for the opportunity to bring such an esteemed author to Gillette.

READ
READ
READ
READ
READ
READ
READ
READ

SUCCEED
NATIONAL LIBRARY WEEK
APRIL 14-20, 1991
American Library Association

WHAT'S HAPPENING IN WRIGHT?

BABYSITTER'S BAG OF TRICKS: 3:30 to 4:30, every Thursday afternoon in April. This program is offered to children age 11 or older. Those attending will learn about safety, first-aid, and how to entertain children. Classes fulfill the Girl Scout babysitter's badge requirements. Pre-registration is required as class size is limited.

NATIONAL LIBRARY WEEK: April 14-20. Be sure to stop in the library for complimentary coffee and muffins.

AFTER-SCHOOL SPECIAL: Wednesday, April 24, 3:30-4:30 p.m. Come learn about Wyoming wildlife. Program will be held in the mall commons area.

SIXTH GRADE OPEN HOUSE: Wednesday, May 15, 3:30-5:00 p.m. All sixth grade students are invited to learn more about the library and watch a fun film while eating fries. It's a big step from sixth grade to seventh, let's take it together.

AFTER-SCHOOL SPECIAL: Wednesday, May 22, 3:30-4:30 p.m. This program, about the wonders of gardening, will be held in the mall commons area.

COME RIDE WITH US ON THE STORYTIME BUS: Thursday mornings, 10:00 to 10:30 a.m.

WRIGHT BRANCH HOURS: Mon., Wed., Thurs.: 9-1 & 2-5
Tues.: 12-7
Fri., Sat.: 10-1
464-0500*In the Latigo Hills Mall

THE DOWNTOWN BRANCH

Be sure to stop in and view the artwork of Campbell County's artists throughout the month of April. The artists will be honored at a public reception at the downtown branch on Monday, April 22, from 7:00 to 9:00 p.m. Come sample the art and the cuisine.

Join in the mystery at the George Amos Branch during National Library Week (April 15-19). Complementary cookies and juice will be served throughout the week. Stop in and find something "mysterious" each day.

MYSTERY PARTY AFTER-SCHOOL SPECIAL: Thursday, April 18, 4:00 to 4:45 p.m. Follow the clues and find the bizarre item. Program includes games, stories, and more.

MOTHER'S DAY AFTER-SCHOOL SPECIAL: Thursday, May 9, 4:00 to 4:45 p.m. Come make a special gift for Mom.

FEATURED MONTHLY ARTISTS:
April - Local Artists Art Show
May - Marte Stines

George Amos Branch & Law Library Hours:
Monday through Friday 1:00 - 5:00 p.m.
412 S. Gillette Ave.*682-2233
(Law Library Assistant in library on Monday & Wednesday)
Law Library Phone: 686-6327

newsline

CAMPBELL COUNTY PUBLIC LIBRARY
2101 4-J Road
Gillette, Wyoming 82716

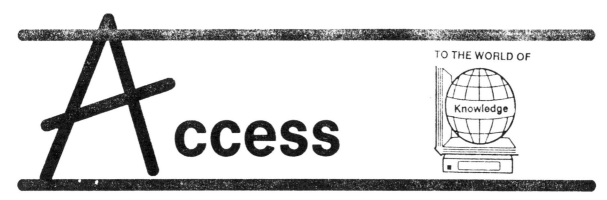

Nicholson Memorial Library System Newsletter

February 1991

1991 - YEAR OF THE LIFETIME READER

First Lady Barbara Bush will serve as honorary chair of "1991 - The Year of the Lifetime Reader," the Library of Congress' new national campaign to remind Americans of the joy and importance of reading as a lifetime activity.

Initiated by the Center of the Book in the Library of Congress, Year of the Lifetime Reader is a unifying theme for supporting reading and literacy projects that benefit all age groups. The campaign encourages and draws attention to family literacy programs, adult literacy and reading motivation projects, and the needs of blind and physically handicapped readers.

1991 - The Year of the Lifetime Reader is supported by business firms, professional and civic organizations, volunteer groups, labor unions, schools, libraries, and others who believe reading is vital to individual fulfillment and democratic society.

-from the Library of Congress *Information Bulletin*.

**GIVE US BOOKS
GIVE US WINGS**

To become a Literacy volunteer contact one of the local agencies listed on the next page.

 ADAMS COUNTY PUBLIC LIBRARY **AD LIB**

Vol. 8, Nos. 3 & 4   **Fall/Winter, 1990**

"YEAR OF THE LIFETIME READER"

BOOKS
GIVE US
WINGS

THE LIBRARY OF CONGRESS
YEAR OF THE LIFETIME READER
1991

Libraries across the country will be celebrating 1991 as "The Year of the Lifetime Reader." The concept of the "Year of the Lifetime Reader" was conceived by the Center for the Book in the Library of Congress to recognize that "an informed and literate citizenry is vital to a strong democracy"* and that "reading helps individuals to meet their responsibilities...by providing personal enjoyment, knowledge and information."* The "Year of the Lifetime Reader" is "aimed at giving our citizens at every age and in every walk of life the gift, joy and promise of reading"* and encourages support for reading and literacy projects for people of all ages.

In conjunction with the "Year of the Lifetime Reader," the ACLS plans to create displays, present a special program or two, and emphasize its Adult Literacy Program. At the moment, ACLS staff at the Commerce City and Thornton Branches are planning to hold a "Night of 1,000 Stars" during National Library Week in April. These programs will focus on the dual theme of National Library Week - "Read. Succeed." and "Kids Who Read Succeed." It will feature various members of the community reading and/or talking about reading.

The ACLS Adult Literacy Program has been teaching adults to improve their reading skills since 1986. If you would like information about the program, or if you are interested in being a participant as either a student or volunteer tutor, contact Ed Stephen at **287-2759.**

*"Year of the Lifetime Reader" Resolution, from the National Center for the Book

1991 SCHEDULE CHANGES

Effective on January 1, 1991, there were two library schedule changes, one at the Commerce City Branch and one on the bookmobile. The Commerce City Branch will now be open on Tuesday mornings instead of Tuesday evenings; and the Cherry Drive bookmobile stop has been cancelled due to lack of use.

As of January 1, 1991,
Commerce City Branch open hours are:

Monday, Thursday   1:00 - 8:00
Tuesday, Wednesday, Friday, Saturday   10:00 - 5:00

The Cherry Drive bookmobile stop is: Cancelled

THOSE INEVITABLE TAXES

All ACLS branches will, once again, be distributing tax forms for the IRS and for the State of Colorado. Individual forms will be available to the extent that they are supplied by the IRS or the State. However, each location has a set of every IRS form for 1991 available for photocopying; so if the form you need is not there for the taking, ask for the notebook of forms - it is generally kept behind the desk.

Library staff are not tax experts or advisers. They suffer the same trauma and uncertainty as you do when it comes to filing. They will be able to tell you whether they have a particular form - and, if they are out of a form, whether they expect to get replacements. But please do not expect them to provide you with advice on such matters as which tax form is appropriate for your purposes, etc.

To help ease you through the 1991 tax season, several branches will be providing "Tax Seminars." These seminars will be presented by members of the Colorado Society of Certified Public Accountants, Taxpayer Assistance Committee. They are essentially question and answer sessions, so bring your tax questions, problems and concerns. All seminars are free and open to the publc. The schedule of seminars is as follows :

Perl Mack Branch
Monday, January 28th   6:30 - 8:00 p.m.
Brighton Branch
Thursday, February 7th   6:30 - 8:00 p.m.
Commerce City Branch
Thursday, February 21st   6:30 - 8:00 p.m.
Thornton Branch
Monday, March 4th   6:30 - 8:00 p.m.

ADAMS COUNTY LIBRARY SYSTEM :
POLICIES and HOURS
- Effective January 1, 1991 -

CARDS

Any resident of Adams County who does *not* live in an Adams County city which has its own library may obtain an ACLS card . If you live outside of Adams County, or in an Adams County city with a municipal library, you will need a card from your local library. Your local card can then be used at the ACLS. There is no charge for your first ACLS library card. If you are a new patron, you will need proof of your Adams County address (a driver's license, or a piece of mail addressed to your Adams County address, will do) and you may register at any ACLS branch or bookmobile. Your ACLS card is good at most metro area libraries.

LOAN PERIODS

Books - 3 weeks, unless otherwise restricted to a shorter loan period
Magazines - 1 week
Vertical File items - 1 week
Audio Visual materials - 1 week
Renewals (from the date on which you make the renewal) - 7 days, for all renewable items

FINES

Branch Charges - 10¢ per day, for most items
- 5¢ for magazines, vertical file items and some paperbacks
- 50¢ per day for certain restricted items, such as encyclopedias and interlibrary loans
Bookmobile Charges - 50¢ between stops
Grace Period (fines are waived if items are returned within this time. Interlibrary loans and some restricted loans are excepted)
- 1 week, for 3 week loans
- 3 days, for most 7 day loans
Maximum Fines - $2.00 for children's materials, except restricted loans
- $2.00 for magazines, vertical file materials, puzzles and some paperbacks
- $5.00 for adult materials, except certain restricted loans
- $5.00 or $10.00 for some restriced loans

OTHER FEES

Processing Charges - $4.00 for books and audio visual materials
- $1.00 for magazines, vertical file materials, and some paperbacks
Deposits - A refundable deposit, a personal item or a signature may be required to check out some items or to use certain items on location
Replacement Library Cards - $1.00
Collection Agency Handling Fee - $10.00
Photocopying Fees - 10¢ per page

BRANCH SCHEDULES

BRIGHTON	575 S. 8th	659-2572	BENNETT	495 7th	644-3303
COMMERCE CITY	7185 Monaco	287-0063	Mon., Thurs.		1:00 - 7:00
PERL MACK	7611 Hilltop Cr.	428-3576	Wed.		12:00 - 5:00
THORNTON	8992 N. Washington	287-2514	Tues., Fri., Sat.		10:00 - 5:00
Mon., Thurs.		1:00 - 8:00			
Tues., Wed., Fri., Sat.		10:00 - 5:00			
NORTHGLENN	10530 N. Huron	452-7534	STRASBURG MINI-BRANCH		
Mon., Tues., Thurs.		10:00 - 8:00	School Parking Lot		622-4268
Wed., Fri., Sat.		10:00 - 5:00	Wed.		10:00 - 5:00

BOOKMOBILE

For information, call 288-2001, or any branch

ADMINISTRATION   ADULT LITERACY

288-2001   8992 North Washington   287-2759
Mon. - Fri.   8:00 - 5:00

If you have a problem or question about overdue notices or materials, you may call Administration during business hours. Or you may contact your branch library.

••

This newsletter is published periodically. We will try to keep you informed of library happenings and issues and, when space allows, to acquaint you with members of the ACLS staff. We hope that you find it informative and we invite your comments, as well as your suggestions for future topics.

1902-1990

TEXAS LIBRARY ASSOCIATION
ORGANIZED TO PROMOTE LIBRARY SERVICE IN TEXAS
Central Office: 3355 Bee Cave Road • Suite 603 • Austin, Texas 78746

NON-PROFIT
U.S. POSTAGE
PAID
AUSTIN, TEXAS
PERMIT NO. 1429

Media Matters

TEXAS ASSOCIATION OF SCHOOL LIBRARIANS   NEWSLETTER

"ABOUT LIBRARIANS AND MEDIA SERVICE IN THE STATE OF TEXAS"   **Winter, 1990**

Editor, Patricia Mulkey, District Library Coordinator, Plano Independent School District

"WORLDS" AWAIT 1991 CONFERENCE GOERS

Unlimited opportunities and infinite variety await conference goers when they step into "Libraries: Worlds of Lifelong Learning" at the 1991 TLA Annual Conference. The gathering, to be held April 9–13 in Ft. Worth at the Tarrant County Convention Center, will offer scintillating speakers, innovative technology, informative exhibits, and enough sparkling entertainment to please the most discriminating tastes.

Keynote speakers Will Manley and Leo Lionni will present perspectives on lives and avocations vastly different, but equally fascinating. Known for his column, "Facing the Public" in Wilson Library Bulletin, Manley is sure to provide a fast–paced and stimulating foray into his personal views on the library world. Lionni, renowned author and illustrator, will bring with him glimpses of a unique sense of design and personal vitality which infuse his work and which have made him universally loved. Both speakers are sure to be "must sees!"

Other guest authors sure to please are Joan Lowery Nixon, Judith St. George, Pam Conrad, and Jon Scieszka. Ms. Nixon will be the guest of YART, speaking on "Mystery to History: Why I write for Teenagers." YART, TASL and CRT will be featuring Ms. St. George, author of The Brooklyn Bridge: They Said It couldn't Be Built, and Mr. Scieszka, author of The True Story of the Three Little Pigs. Their creative approaches to writing for children and young adults make this a special event not to be missed! Author of Prairie Songs and My Daniel, Pam Conrad, will share her talents with Children's Round Table.

There are many, many more programs and events that will round out the conference schedule. Stay tuned to this space for more previews and tips concerning "worlds" of exciting opportunities waiting for you at the 1991 TLA Conference!

Night Of A 1000 Stars will be a nation–wide observance during National Library Week in April 1991. Plan a special event in your library during that week. Your celebration may be during the day, after school or at night. It may take place in your library, in classrooms, in the cafeteria or the auditorium.

Celebrities invited to read may be:
  teachers or teachers' spouses
  principals
  central office administrators
  librarians
  junior college, college or university administrators,
  professors or athletes
  school board members
  city council members
  other elected officials
  community leaders
  television and/or radio personalities
  local authors
  storytellers
  high school students
  custodial or cafeteria workers

Make your initial contact to celebrities by telephone. Follow up your call with a letter of confirmation. After your celebration, send a hand–written thank you note.

PUBLICITY SUGGESTIONS

Use a tie–in with ALA's national celebration stressing the importance of families reading together.

Send or hand carry informational letters promoting your activities to local newspapers, TV stations, school district publicity office and radio stations. Include all information concerning the event plus the name and telephone number of a contact person.

Enlist PTA members to provide items to create a home–like atmosphere — rocking chairs, area rugs, etc.

Provide handouts with suggestions which encourage families to take the time to read together.

TV and newspaper coverage more readily follows if you include guest readers from TV and newspapers.

The following ideas for Night Of A 1000 Stars were submitted by librarians from around the state based on their celebration in April 1990.

Come in your pajamas and bring your favorite "cuddly" for a bedtime story and milk and cookies.

Kathi Dalton, Bushy Creek Elementary, Round Rock ISD

Prepare choral readings from library books. Children performing promotes attendance.

Debbie Whitbeck, Purple Sage Elem., Round Rock ISD

Allow time for children to ask questions of guest readers.

Dee Cameron, Burnett Library, El Paso ISD

Group schools into community clusters (feeder clusters and have some meetings in elementary schools and some in secondary schools.

Joan Leach, Fort Worth ISD

Send guests to classrooms during the school day to read to students.

Linda Williams, Del Norte Heights Elementary, Ysleta ISD

Involve students in publicizing the event by making bookmarks, posters, mobiles and banners.

Nancy Newton, Roscoe Wilson Elementary, Lubbock ISD

D.E.A.R. B.E.A.R. (Drop Everything And Read—Be Enthusiastic About Reading a read–in sleep–in) First graders brought bedrolls and spent the night in the library with guest readers. GREEN EGGS AND HAM was read before serving the children breakfast the next morning.

Connie Healer, Bebensee Elementary, Arlington ISD

Celebrate Week of XXX (number of students in school) Stars. Each students lists their name and favorite book on a star to be displayed.

Linda Fowler, Blanton Elementary, Arlington ISD

Prepare a poster to use as a frame in which children can sit with their favorite book. Make photographs and use them in a display.

Jan Thomas, Workman Elementary, Arlington ISD

Ask celebrity readers to talk about the importance of reading in addition to reading aloud. Ask celebrities to sign stars for a "Wall of Fame".

Becky Menti, Key Elementary, Arlington ISD

Ask the guest reader to read for 15 minutes, then the guest and students read silently for 15 minutes. Students may bring pillows for the read–in.

Twila Forbes, Hardwick Elementary, Lubbock ISD

Make a presentation to PTA on the importance of parents reading to/with children.

Judy Burnett, Wheelock Elementary, Lubbock ISD

Schedule your celebration immediately after school.

Doris Mullican, Whiteside Elementary, Lubbock ISD

Be a "Parent Reading Star" — Invite parents to read a favorite book to their child's class during NLW.

Barbara Stanford, Guadalupe Elementary, Lubbock ISD

Schedule sixth grade students to read to first grade students.

Dru Castleman, Bayless Elementary, Lubbock ISD

Celebrate Month Of A Thousand Stars in April. Every teacher, student and staff member turns in the title of all books read. Set a goal for your building and prepare a display recognizing readers. A Read–in Lock–in for junior high students raised more than $300 to purchase library books for schools in Honduras. Students secured pledges (.25 to 3.00 per hour) for each hour they were able to read. A break was planned at the end of each two–hour reading session.

Dorothy Wiseman, Bailey Junior High, Arlington ISD

Assign your guest readers to classrooms which students have decorated based on the readers' selections. Attendees can be rotated to the classrooms.

Diane Garland, Oakwilde Elementary, Aldine ISD

March, 1991   Volume 11, No. 2

in the know

**A Publication of the
Pasadena Public Library**

Focus On:
National Women's History Month
WOMEN, WAR, AND PEACE
(See Story on Page 1)

Mailed by

FRIENDS OF THE PASADENA
PUBLIC LIBRARY
285 East Walnut
Pasadena, California 91101

In the Know
Staff

Edited and written by the
Newsletter Committee:
Susan Kalendrut
Bill LaHay
Reference Services
Pamela Groves
Rosa Martin
Sally Martin
Donna A. Watkins
Public Services
Steve Gazanian
Support Services
Shirley Mauller
Shirley Singleton
Friends of the Library

Additional articles
contributed by
Rosemarie Roen
Mary Williams

Guest columnist
D.P. Roy Myers

Layout and production
Vendi Elmen

Typesetting
Fotocraft

Printing
Glendale Rotary Press

APPENDIX E

1991 GRAMMAR HOTLINE DIRECTORY

The *Grammar Hotline Directory* lists telephone services that provide free answers to short questions about writing, grammar, punctuation, spelling, diction, and syntax. Most of these services are staffed by faculty members, graduate students, and retired teachers.

Information for the directory is provided by the services listed. Changes may occur during the year, and hours of operation vary according to teaching schedules. Most of the hotlines either reduce or suspend service during college breaks and summer terms. Unless noted otherwise, services will not accept collect calls and will return long-distance calls collect only.

For each free copy of the directory, send a self-addressed, stamped (first-class postage), business-letter-size envelope to *Grammar Hotline Directory*, Tidewater Community College Writing Center, 1700 College Crescent, Virginia Beach, VA 23456. For further information, contact Donna Reiss, Writing Center/Grammar Hotline Director, (804) 427-7170.

Alabama

AUBURN 36849
(205)844-5749 -- Writing Center Hotline
Monday through Wednesday, 9:00 a.m. to
noon and 1:00 p.m. to 4:00 p.m.; Thursday, 1:00 p.m.
to 4:00 p.m.; Friday, 8:00 a.m. to noon.
Auburn University
Lex Williford

JACKSONVILLE 36265
(205) 782-5409 -- Grammar Hotline
Monday through Friday, 8:00 a.m. to 4:30
p.m.
Jacksonville State University
Carol Cauthen and Clyde Cox

TUSCALOOSA 35487-1438
(205) 348-5049 -- Grammar Hotline
Monday through Thursday, 8:30 a.m. to
4:00 p.m.; Tuesday and Wednesday, 6:00 p.m. to 9:00
p.m.; Friday, 8:30 a.m. to 1:00 p.m.
University of Alabama
Carol Howell

Arizona

TEMPE 85287
(602) 921-3616 (residence) -- Grammar
Hotline
Daily 6:00 a.m. to 10:00 p.m.
Arizona State University, Professor Emeritus
J.J. Lamberts

Arkansas

LITTLE ROCK 72204
(501) 569-3162 -- The Writer's Hotline
Monday through Friday, 8:00 a.m. to noon
University of Arkansas at Little Rock
Marilynn Keys

California

MOORPARK 93021
(805) 529-2321 -- National Grammar Hotline
Monday through Friday, 8:00 a.m. to noon,
September through June
Moorpark College
Michael Strumpf

SACRAMENTO 95823-5799
(916) 688-7444 -- English Helpline
Monday through Friday, 9:00 a.m. to 11:45
a.m., fall and spring semesters; 24-hour answering
machine
Cosumnes River College
Billie Miller Cooper

Colorado

PUEBLO 81001
(719) 549-2787 -- USC Grammar Hotline
Monday through Friday, 9:30 a.m. to 3:30 p.m.
University of Southern Colorado
Margaret Senatore and Ralph Dille

Delaware

NEWARK 19716
(312) 451-1890 Grammar Hotline
Monday through Thursday, 9:00 a.m. to noon, 1:00 p.m.
to 5:00 p.m., and 6:00 p.m. to 9:00 p.m.; Friday, 9:00
a.m. to noon and 1:00 p.m. to 5:00 p.m.
University of Delaware
Margaret P. Hassert

Florida

CORAL GABLES 33124
(305) 284-2956 -- Grammar Hotline
Monday through Friday, 8:30 a.m. to 5:00 p.m.; Monday
and Thursday, to 8:30 p.m.
University of Miami
Charlotte Perlin

PENSACOLA 32514
(904) 474-2129 -- Writing Lab and Grammar Hotline
Monday through Thursday 9:00 a.m. to 5:00 p.m.;
occasional evening hours
University of West Florida
Mamie Webb Hixon

Georgia

ATLANTA 30303
(404) 651-2906 -- Writing Center
Monday through Friday, 8:30 a.m. to 5:00 p.m.; evening
hours vary
Georgia State University
Patricia Graves

ROME 30162-1864
(404) 295-6312 -- Grammar Hotline
Monday through Friday, 8:30 a.m. to 5:00 p.m.
Floyd College
Philip Dillard

Illinois

CHARLESTON 61920
(217) 581-5929 -- Grammar Hotline
Monday through Friday, 10:00 a.m. to 3:00 p.m.
Eastern Illinois University
Linda S. Coleman

DES PLAINES 60016
(708) 635-1948 -- The Write Line
Monday through Friday, 9:30 a.m. to 3:00 p.m.
Oakton Community College
Richard Francis Tracz

NORMAL 61761
(309) 438-2345 -- Grammar Hotline
Monday through Friday, 8:00 a.m. to 4:30 p.m.
Illinois State University
Janice Neuleib

OGLESBY 61761
(815) 224-2720 -- Grammarline
Monday through Friday, 8:00 a.m. to 4:00 p.m.
Illinois Valley Community College
Robert Howard and Robert Mueller

PALATINE 60067-7398
(708) 397-3000, ext. 2389 -- Grammar "Right" Line
24-hour answering machine; calls returned Monday
through Friday, 9:00 a.m. to 1:00 p.m.
William Rainey Harper College
Doris Howden and Nimi Tobaa

RIVER GROVE 60171
(708) 456-0300, ext. 254 -- Grammar phone
Monday through Thursday, 8:00 a.m. to 8:00 p.m.;
Friday, 8:00 a.m. to 3:00 p.m.; Saturday, 9:00 a.m. to
1:00 p.m.
Triton College
Natalie Nemeth

Indiana

INDIANAPOLIS 46202
(317) 274-3000 - IUPUI Writing Center Hotline
Monday through Thursday, 9:00 a.m. to 5:00 p.m.;
Friday and Saturday, 9:00 a.m. to 2:00 p.m.
Indian University-Purdue University at Indianapolis,
University Writing Center
Barbara Cambridge

MUNCIE 47306
(317) 285-8387 -- Grammar Crisis Line
Monday through Thursday, 9:00 a.m. to 8:00 p.m.;
Friday, 9:00 a.m. to 5:00 p.m., September through
May; Monday through Friday, 11:00 a.m. to 2:00
p.m., May through August
Ball State University, The Writing Center
Paul W. Ranieri

WEST LAFAYETTE 47907
(317) 494-3723 -- Grammar Hotline
Monday through Friday, 9:30 a.m. to 4:00 p.m.; closed
May, August, and mid-December to Mid-January
Purdue University
Muriel Harris

Kansas

EMPORIA 66801
(316) 343-5380 -- Writer's Hotline
Monday through Thursday, noon to 4:00 p.m.;
Wednesday and Thursday, 7:00 p.m. to 10:00 p.m.;
answering machine
Emporia State University
see KANSAS CITY, MISSOURI

Louisiana

LAFAYETTE 70504-4691
(318) 231-5224 -- Grammar Hotline
Monday through Thursday, 8:00 a.m. to 4:00 p.m.;
   Friday, 8:00 a.m. to 3:00 p.m.
University of Southwestern Louisiana
James McDonald

Maryland

BALTIMORE 21228
(301) 455-2585 -- Writer's hotline
Monday through Friday, 10:00 a.m. to noon, September
   through May
University of Maryland Baltimore County
Barbara Cooper

FROSTBURG 21532
(301) 689-4327 -- Grammarphone (patented trademark)
Monday through Friday, 10:00 a.m. to noon
Frostburg State University English Department
Glynn Baugher

Massachusetts

LYNN 01901
(617) 593-7284 -- Grammar Hotline
Monday through Friday, 8:30 a.m. to 4:00 p.m.
North Shore Community College
Marilyn Dorfman

BOSTON 02115
(617) 437-2512 -- Grammar Hotline
Monday through Friday, 8:30 a.m. to 4:30 p.m.
Northeastern University English Department
Stuart Peterfreund

Michigan

FLINT 48503
(313) 762-0229 -- Grammar Hotline
Monday through Thursday, 8:30 a.m. to 3:30 p.m.;
   Friday, 8:30 a.m. to 12:30 p.m.; Tuesday and
   Wednesday, 5:30 p.m. to 8:30 p.m.
C.S. Mott Community College
Leatha Terwilliger

KALAMAZOO 49008-5031
(616) 387-4442 -- Writer's Hotline
Monday through Friday, 9:00 a.m. to 4:00 p.m.
Lansing Community College
George R. Bramer

Missouri

JOPLIN 64801
(417) 624-0171 -- Grammar Hotline
Monday through Friday, 8:30 a.m. to 4:30 p.m.
Missouri Southern State College
Dale W. Simpson

KANSAS CITY 64110-2499
(816) 235-2244 -- Writer's Hotline
Monday through Friday, 9:00 a.m. to 4:00 p.m.
University of Missouri-Kansas City
Judy McCormick, David Foster, and Karen Doerr

New Jersey

JERSEY CITY 07305
(201) 547-3337 or -3338 -- Grammar Hotline
Monday through Friday, 9:00 a.m. to 4:30 p.m.; summer
   Monday through Thursday, 8:00   a.m. to 5:00 p.m.
Jersey City State College
Harlan Hamilton

New York

JAMAICA 11451
(718) 739-7483 -- Rewrite
Monday through Friday, 1:00 p.m. to 4:00 p.m.
York College of the City University of New York
Joan Baum and Alan Cooper

North Carolina

FAYETTEVILLE 28311
(919) 488-7110 -- Grammar hotline
Monday through Friday, 9:00 a.m. to 4:00 p.m.
Methodist College
Robert Christian, Sue L. Kimball, and James X. Ward

GREENVILLE 27858
(919) 757-6728 or 757-6399 -- Grammar Hotline
Monday through Thursday, 8:00 a.m. to 4:00 p.m.;
 Friday, 8:00 a.m. to 3:00 p.m.; Tuesday and
 Thursday, 6:00 p.m. to 9:00 p.m.
East Carolina University
Jo Allen

Ohio

CINCINNATI 45236
(513) 745-5731 -- Dial-A-Grammar
Tapes request -- returns calls
Raymond Walters College
Phyllis A. Sherwood

CINCINNATI 45221
(513) 556-1702 -- Writer's Remedies
Monday, Wednesday, and Friday 9:00 a.m. to 10:00 a.m.
 and noon to 2:00 p.m.; Tuesday and Thursday,
 11:00 a.m. to noon
University College, University of Cincinnati
Jay A. Yarmove

CINCINNATI 45223
(513) 569-1736 or 569-1737 -- Writing Center Hotline
Monday through Thursday, 8:00 a.m. to 8:00 p.m.;
 Friday, 8:00 a.m. to 4:00 p.m.; Saturday, 9:00 a.m. to
 1:00 p.m.
Cincinnati Technical College
John Battistone and Catherine Rahmes

CLEVELAND 44122-6195
(216) 987-2050 -- Grammar Hotline
Monday through Friday, 1:00 p.m. to 3:00 p.m.; Sunday
 through Thursday, 7:00 p.m. to 10:00 p.m.; 24-hour
 answering machine
Cuyahoga Community College
Margaret Taylor, Norman Prange, and Susan Marsick

DAYTON 45435
(513) 873-2158 -- Writer's Hotline
Monday through Friday, 9:00 a.m. to 4:00 p.m.
Wright State University
Maura Taaffe

DELAWARE 43015
(614) 368-3925 -- Writing Resource Center
Monday through Friday, 9:00 a.m. to noon and 1:00 p.m.
 to 4:00 p.m., September through April; answers both
 written and telephoned questions
Ohio Wesleyan University
Ulle Lewes and Barbara Pinkele

Oklahoma

BETHANY 73008
(405) 491-6328 -- Grammar Hotline
Monday through Friday, 9:00 a.m. to 4:00 p.m.; June,
 July, and August call (405) 354-1739
Southern Nazarene University
Jim Wilcox

CHICKASHA 73018
(405) 224-8622
Monday through Friday, 9:00 a.m. to 5:00 p.m.;
 Saturday, 9:00 a.m. to noon.
Mrs. Underwood, retired teacher and editor, offers this
 service through her home telephone.
Virginia Lee Underwood

Pennsylvania

ALLENTOWN 18104-6196
(215) 437-4471 -- Academic Support Center
Monday through Friday, 10:00 a.m. to 3:00 p.m.,
 September through May
Cedar Crest College

GLEN MILLS 19342
(215) 399-1130 -- Burger Associates
Monday through Friday, 9:00 a.m. to 5:00 p.m.
Mr. Burger, formerly a teacher of writing and journalism
 at several colleges, offers this service through his
 office, which conducts courses in effective writing.
Robert S. Burger

LINCOLN UNIVERSITY 19352
(215) 932-8300, ext. 460 -- Grammar Hotline
Monday through Friday, 9:00 a.m. to 5:00 p.m.,
 September through May
Lincoln University
Carolyn L. Simpson

South Carolina

CHARLESTON 29409
(803) 792-3194 -- Writer's Hotline
Monday through Friday, 8:00 a.m. to 4:00 p.m.; Sunday
through Thursday, 7:00 p.m. to 10:00 p.m.
The Citadel Writing Center
Angela W. Williams

COLUMBIA 29208
(803) 777-7020 -- Writer's Hotline
Monday through Thursday, 8:30 a.m. to 5:00 p.m.;
Friday, 8:30 a.m. to 4:00 p.m.
University of South Carolina Writing Center
Nancy Butterworth and Suzanne Moore

SPARTANBURG 29301
(803) 596-9613 -- Writer's Hotline
Monday through Thursday, 1:00 p.m. to 6:00 p.m.;
Wednesday, 7:30 a.m. to 9:00 p.m.
Converse College Writing Center
Bonnie Auslander

Texas

AMARILLO 79178-0001
(806) 374-4726 -- Grammarphone
Monday through Thursday, 8:00 a.m. to 9:00 p.m.;
Friday, 8:00 a.m. to 3:00 p.m.; Sunday, 2:00 p.m. to
6:00 p.m.
Amarillo College
Patricia Maddox and Carl Fowler

HOUSTON 77002
(713) 221-8670 -- University of Houston Downtown
Grammar Line
Monday through Thursday, 9:00 a.m. to 4:00 p.m.;
Friday, 9:00 a.m. to 1:00 p.m.; summer hours,
Monday through Thursday, 10:30 a.m. to 4:00 p.m.
University of Houston Downtown
Linda Coblentz

SAN ANTONIO 78284
(512) 733-2503 -- Dial-a-Tutor
Monday through Thursday, 8:00 a.m. to 9:00 p.m.;
Friday, 8:00 a.m. to 4:00 p.m.
San Antonio College Learning Lab
Irma Luna and Jane Focht-Hansen

Virginia

STERLING 22170
(703) 450-2511 -- Writing Center
Monday through Thursday, 10:00 a.m. to 2:00 p.m.
Northern Virginia Community College
Loudoun Campus

VIRGINIA BEACH 23456
(804) 427-7170 -- Grammar Hotline
Monday through Friday, 10:00 a.m. to noon; afternoon
and evening hours vary
Tidewater Community College
Donna Reiss

West Virginia

MONTGOMERY 25136
(304) 442-3137 -- Writer's Hotline
Monday through Thursday, 9:30 a.m. to 4:00 p.m.; 24
hour answering machine
West Virginia Institute of Technology
Eva Kay Cardea

Wisconsin

GREEN BAY 54307-9042
(414) 498-5427 -- Grammar Hotline
Monday through Thursday, 8:30 a.m. to 8:00 p.m.;
Friday, 8:30 a.m. to 4:00 p.m.; summer hours, Friday,
8:30 a.m. to noon
Northeast Wisconsin Technical College
Rose Marie Mastricola and Joanne Rathburn

PLATTEVILLE 53818
(608) 342-1615 -- Grammar Hotline
Monday through Thursday, 9:00 a.m. to 4:00 p.m.;
Friday, 9:00 a.m. to noon
University of Wisconsin-Platteville
Sheri Lindquist

Canada

EDMONTON, ALBERTA T5J2P2
(403) 441-4699 -- Grammar Hotline
Monday through Thursday, 9:00 a.m. to 11:00 a.m. and
1:00 p.m. to 3:00 p.m.
Grant MacEwan Community College
Lois Drew

FREDERICTON, NEW BRUNSWICK E3B5A3
(506) 459-3631 (residence) or (506) 453-4666
(university) -- Grammar Hotline
Variable hours
University of New Brunswick
A.M. Kinloch

INDEX

Barbara Radke Blake is a Marketing Representative with AMIGOS. She was formerly Faculty Associate at the University of Texas Southwestern Medical Center in Dallas, and before that worked several years as a public librarian.

Barbara L. Stein is Associate Professor at the School of Library and Information Science at the University of North Texas. She has experience both as a school teacher and a media specialist.

CREATING NEWSLETTERS, BROCHURES, AND PAMPHLETS

A How-To-Do-It Manual

KE

BRARIANS

, INC.

Published by Neal-Schuman Publishers, Inc.
100 Varick Street
New York, NY 10013

Printed and bound in the United States of America

Library of Congress Cataloging-in-Publication Data

Blake, Barbara Radke
    Creating newsletters, brochures, and pamphlets : a how-to-do-it
manual / Barbara Radke Blake, Barbara L. Stein.
       p.   cm. — (How-to-do-it manuals for school and public
librarians ;no. 2)
    Includes bibliographical references and index.
    ISBN 1-55570-107-8
    1. Libraries—Publishing—Handbooks, manuals, etc.
2. Advertising—Libraries—Handbooks, manuals, etc. 3. Public
relations—Libraries—Handbooks, manuals, etc.   4. Newsletters—
Publishing—Handbooks, manuals, etc.   5. Pamphlets—Publishing—
Handbooks, manuals, etc.   I. Stein, Barbara L.   II. Title.
III. Series.
Z716.6.R3   1992
070.5′94—dc20   92-1370
                                                     CIP